Volume 2

The National Diet & Nutrition Survey: adults aged 19 to 64 years

Energy, protein, carbohydrate, fat and alcohol intake

Lynne Henderson
Jan Gregory
Karen Irving
Office for National Statistics

with **Gillian Swan**
Food Standards Agency

A survey carried out in Great Britain on behalf of the Food Standards Agency and the Departments of Health by the Social Survey Division of the Office for National Statistics and Medical Research Council Human Nutrition Research

London: TSO

ISBN 0 11 621567 4

Contact points

For enquiries about this publication, contact
Lynne Henderson
Tel: **020 7533 5385**
E-mail: **lynne.henderson@ons.gov.uk**

To order this publication, call TSO
on **0870 600 5522**. See also inside back cover.

For general enquiries, contact the National Statistics
Customer Enquiry Centre on **0845 601 3034**
(minicom: 01633 812399)
E-mail: **info@statistics.gov.uk**
Fax: 01633 652747
Letters: Room D.115, Government Buildings,
Cardiff Road, Newport NP10 8XG

You can also find National Statistics on the Internet
at **www.statistics.gov.uk**

About the Office for National Statistics

The Office for National Statistics (ONS) is the government
agency responsible for compiling, analysing and disseminating
many of the United Kingdom's economic, social and
demographic statistics, including the retail prices index, trade
figures and labour market data, as well as the periodic census of
the population and health statistics. The Director of ONS is also
the National Statistician and the Registrar General for England
and Wales, and the agency administers the statutory registration
of births, marriages and deaths there.

This report has been produced by the Social Survey Division of
the Office for National Statistics in accordance with the Official
Statistics Code of Practice.

Contents

Foreword

This survey, of a national sample of adults aged 19 to 64 years, is one of a programme of national surveys with the aim of gathering information about the dietary habits and nutritional status of the British population. The results of the survey will be used to develop nutrition policy and to contribute to the evidence base for Government advice on healthy eating.

This report, covering intakes of energy and macronutrients, is the second in a series on the findings of this survey. The first report, covering foods consumed, was published in December 2002. Further reports on micronutrient intakes and nutritional status will be published during 2003.

The work described in this series of reports results from a successful collaboration between the Food Standards Agency and the Department of Health, who jointly funded the collection of the survey data, with the Office for National Statistics and the Medical Research Council Human Nutrition Research.

We warmly welcome this second report of the latest survey in the National Diet and Nutrition Survey programme and express our thanks to all the respondents who took part.

Sir John Krebs
Chairman
Food Standards Agency

Hazel Blears
Minister for Public Health
Department of Health

Authors' acknowledgements

We would like to thank everyone who contributed to the survey and the production of this report:

- the respondents without whose co-operation the survey would not have been possible;

- the interviewers of Social Survey Division of ONS who recruited the respondents and carried out all the fieldwork stages of the survey;

- colleagues in Social Survey Division of ONS in the Sampling Implementation Unit, Field Branch, Business Solutions, Methodology Unit and Project Support Branch, in particular, Amanda Wilmot, Jo Bacon, Bev Botting, Ann Whitby, Michaela Pink, Caroline Ojemuyiwa, Michael Staley, Glenn Edy, Andrew Tollington, Dave Elliot, Jeremy Barton, Tracie Goodfellow and Jacqueline Hoare;

- the ONS nutritionists, namely Debbie Hartwell, Michaela Davies, Sui Yip, Laura Hopkins, Jessica Ive, Sarah Oyston, Claire Jaggers and Robert Anderson;

- the ONS editors, namely Angela Harris, Carole Austen, Mike Donovan, Nina Hall, Sue Heneghan, Sarah Kelly, Dave Philpot, Colin Wakeley, Carol Willis and Heather Yates;

- staff of the Medical Research Council Human Nutrition Research (HNR), particularly Steve Austin, Dr Chris Bates, Dr Andy Coward, Dr Jayne Perks and Dr Ann Prentice;

- Dr Maureen Birch, the survey doctor, for her input into the design, conduct and interpretation of the survey, in particular for her negotiations with NHS Local Research Ethics Committees;

- the phlebotomists and local laboratory personnel who were recruited by HNR to take the blood samples, and process and store the blood specimens;

- Professor Elaine Gunter, Chief, National Health and Nutrition Examination Survey (NHANES) Laboratory, Centres for Disease Control and Prevention, Atlanta, USA, for an independent review of the methodology for the blood sample collection and laboratory analyses;

- Professor Angus Walls for his contribution to the oral health component and briefing the interviewers on the procedures for the self-tooth and amalgam-filling count;

- Professor Chris Skinner and Dr David Holmes at the University of Southampton for an independent review of response to this NDNS and an assessment of non-response bias;

- David Marker at Westat for an independent review of NDNS methodology and procedures;

- the professional staff at the Food Standards Agency and the Department of Health, in particular Jamie Blackshaw, Susan Church, Michael Day, Melanie Farron, Tom Murray, Dr John Pascoe, Dr Roger Skinner and Alette Weaver of the Food Standards Agency; Richard Bond, Tony Boucher, Ian Cooper, Dr Sheela Reddy and Robert Wenlock of the Department of Health.

Notes to the tables

Tables showing percentages

In general, percentages are shown if the base is 30 or more. Where a base number is less than 30, actual numbers are shown within square brackets.

The row or column percentages may add to 99% or 101% because of rounding and weighting.

The varying positions of the bases in the tables denote the presentation of different types of information. Where the base is at the foot of the table, the whole distribution is presented and the individual percentages add to between 99% and 101%. Where the base is given in a column, the figures refer to the proportion of respondents who had the attribute being discussed, and the complementary proportion, to add to 100%, is not shown in the table.

In tables showing cumulative percentages the row labelled 'All' is always shown as 100%. The proportion of cases falling above the upper limit of the previous band can be calculated by subtracting from 100 the proportion in the previous band. Actual maximum values are not shown in tables of cumulative percentages, since they could vary for different subgroups being considered within the same tables.

Unless shown as a separate group, or stated in the text or a footnote to a table, estimates have been calculated for the total number of respondents in the subgroup, excluding those not answering. Base numbers shown in the tables are the total number of respondents in the subgroup, including those not answering.

The total column may include cases from small subgroups not shown separately elsewhere on the tables, therefore the individual column bases may not add to the base in the total column.

Conventions

The following conventions have been used in the tables:

..	data not available
-	category not applicable; no cases
0	values less than 0.5%
[ ]	numbers inside square brackets are the actual numbers of cases, when the base is fewer than 30.

Tables showing descriptive statistics – mean, percentiles, standard deviation

These are shown in tables to an appropriate number of decimal places.

Significant differences

Differences commented on in the text are shown as being significant at the 95% or 99% confidence levels ($p < 0.05$ and $p < 0.01$). Throughout this volume, the terms 'significant' and 'statistically significant' are used interchangeably. Where differences are shown or described as being 'not statistically significant' or 'ns' this indicates $p > 0.05$. The formulae used to test for significant differences are given in Appendix A, pages 83-89.

Real statistical significance is lower than indicated because all results have been 'trawled' for those showing pairwise statistical significance which increases the likelihood of false significance being indicated.

Where differences between subgroups are compared for a number of variables, for example differences between respondents in different age groups in mean daily energy intake, the significance level shown ($p < 0.05$ or $p < 0.01$) applies to all comparisons, unless otherwise stated.

Standard deviations

Standard deviations for estimates of mean values are shown in the tables and have been calculated for a simple random sample design. In testing for the significant difference between two sample estimates, proportions or means, the sampling error calculated as for a simple random design was multiplied by an assumed design factor of 1.5, to allow for the complex sample design. The reader is referred to Appendix A for an account of the method of calculating true standard errors and for tables of design factors for the main variables and subgroups used throughout this volume. In general, design factors were below 1.5. Therefore although not commented on in the text, there will be some differences in sample proportions and means, that are significantly different, at least at the $p < 0.05$ level.

Weighting

Unless otherwise stated, all proportions and means presented in the tables in the substantive chapters in this volume are taken from data weighted to compensate for the differential probabilities of selection and non-response. Base numbers are presented weighted. All base numbers are given in italics. *See* Appendix B for unweighted base numbers, and Appendix D of the Technical Report online for more details on the weighting: accessible at http://www.food.gov.uk/science.

1 Background, research design and response

This volume presents findings on energy and macronutrient intakes from a survey of the diet and nutrition of adults aged 19 to 64 years living in private households in Great Britain, carried out between July 2000 and June 2001. It is the second volume in a series that will cover food and nutrient intake data derived from the analyses of dietary records, and data on nutritional status from physical measurements including anthropometric data, blood pressure, physical activity and the analyses of blood and urine samples[1]. This first chapter of the volume describes the background to the National Diet and Nutrition Survey (NDNS) of adults aged 19 to 64 years, its main aims, research designs and methodologies and response. Chapter 2 reports on energy intakes. Intakes of carbohydrates and protein are given in Chapter 3, alcohol in Chapter 4 and fat and fatty acids in Chapter 5. Differences are considered by age, sex, region and household receipt of benefits. Chapter 6 presents comparative data from the Dietary and Nutritional Survey of British Adults aged 16 to 64 years, the last survey of this age group[2]. Throughout these chapters, actual intakes are compared with UK Dietary Reference Values, where appropriate.

The Technical Report containing the methodological chapters and appendices is available online[3]. Like previous surveys in the NDNS programme, following publication of the final summary volume, a copy of the survey database, containing the full data set will be deposited with The Data Archive at the University of Essex. Independent researchers who wish to carry out their own analyses should apply to the Archive for access[4].

1.1 The National Diet and Nutrition Survey Programme

The survey forms part of the National Diet and Nutrition Survey programme, which was set up jointly by the Ministry of Agriculture, Fisheries and Food (MAFF)[5] and the Department of Health in 1992 following the successful Dietary and Nutritional Survey of British Adults aged 16 to 64 years carried out in 1986/87 (1986/87 Adults Survey)[2]. MAFF's responsibility for the NDNS programme has now transferred to the Food Standards Agency.

The NDNS programme aims to provide comprehensive, cross-sectional information on the dietary habits and nutritional status of the population of Great Britain. The results of the surveys within the programme are used to develop nutrition policy at a national and local level, and to contribute to the evidence base for Government advice on healthy eating.

The NDNS programme is intended to:

- provide detailed quantitative information on the food and nutrient intakes, sources of nutrients and nutritional status of the population under study as a basis for Government policy;

- describe the characteristics of individuals with intakes of specific nutrients that are above and below the national average;

- provide a database to enable the calculation of likely dietary intakes of natural toxicants, contaminants, additives and other food chemicals for risk assessment;

- measure blood and urine indices that give evidence of nutritional status or dietary biomarkers and to relate these to dietary, physiological and social data;

- provide height, weight and other measurements of body size on a representative sample of individuals and examine their relationship to social, dietary, health and anthropometric data as well as data from blood analyses;

- monitor the diet of the population under study to establish the extent to which it is adequately nutritious and varied;

- monitor the extent of deviation of the diet of specified groups of the population from that recommended by independent experts as optimum for health, in order to act as a basis for policy development;

- help determine possible relationships between diet and nutritional status and risk factors in later life;

- assess physical activity levels of the population under study; and

- provide information on oral health in relation to dietary intake and nutritional status.

The NDNS programme consists of a planned programme of cross-sectional surveys of representative samples of defined age groups of the population. The surveys of older adults, pre-school children, and young people have been published[6,7,8]. The last national survey of diet and nutrition in adults was the 1986/87 Adults Survey[2].

1.2 The sample design and selection

A nationally representative sample of adults aged 19 to 64 years living in private households was required. The sample was selected using a multi-stage random probability design with postal sectors as first stage units. The sampling frame included all postal sectors within mainland Great Britain; selections were made from the small users' Postcode Address File. The frame was stratified by 1991 Census variables. A total of 152 postal sectors was selected as first stage units, with probability proportional to the number of postal delivery points, and 38 sectors were allocated to each of four fieldwork waves. The allocation took account of the need to have approximately equal numbers of households in each wave of fieldwork and for each wave to be nationally representative. From each postal sector 40 addresses were randomly selected[9].

Eligibility was defined as being aged between 19 and 64 and not pregnant or breastfeeding at the time of the doorstep sift[10]. Where there was more than one adult between the ages of 19 and 64 years living in the same household, only one was selected at random to take part in the survey[11]. A more detailed account of the sample design is given in Appendix D of the Technical Report[3]. In keeping with the Social Survey Division of ONS (SSD) normal fieldwork procedures, a letter was sent to each household in the sample in advance of the interviewer calling, telling them briefly about the survey (see Appendix A of the Technical Report[3]).

As in previous surveys in the NDNS series, fieldwork covered a 12-month period, to cover any seasonality in eating behaviour and in the nutrient content of foods; for example, full fat milk. The 12-month fieldwork period was divided into four fieldwork waves, each of three months duration[12]. The fieldwork waves were:

Wave 1: July to September 2000

Wave 2: October to December 2000

Wave 3: January to March 2001

Wave 4: April to June 2001

Feasibility work carried out between September and December 1999 by the SSD and the Medical Research Council Human Nutrition Research (HNR) tested all the components of the survey and made recommendations for revisions for the mainstage. For a subgroup of the feasibility study sample, the validity of the dietary recording methodology was tested using the doubly labelled water methodology to compare energy expenditure against reported energy intake. Further details of the design and results of the feasibility study are summarised in Appendix C of the Technical Report[3].

Ethics approval was gained for the feasibility and mainstage survey from a Multi-centre Research Ethics Committee (MREC), and National Health Service Local Research Ethics Committees covering each of the 152 sampled areas (see Appendix N of the Technical Report[3]).

1.3 The components of the survey

The survey design included: an interview to provide information about the socio-demographic circumstances of the respondent and their household, medication and eating and drinking habits; a weighed dietary record of all food and drink consumed over seven consecutive days; a record of bowel movements for the same seven days; a record of physical activity over the same seven days; physical measurements of the respondent (height, weight, waist and hip circumferences); blood pressure measurements; and a request for a sample of blood and a 24-hour urine collection. Respondents were also asked to do a self-count of the number of teeth and amalgam fillings they had, and provide a sample of tap water from the home for analysis of fluoride.

1.3.1 The dietary and post-dietary record interview

The interview comprised two parts. An initial face-to-face interview using computer-assisted personal interviewing methods (CAPI) to collect information about the respondent's household, their usual dietary behaviour, consumption of artificial sweeteners, herbal teas and other drinks; any foods that were avoided and the reasons for doing so, including vegetarianism and dieting behaviours; the use of salt at the table and in cooking; and the use of fluoride preparations and dietary supplements. Information was also collected on: the respondent's health status; their smoking and drinking habits; socio-economic characteristics; and, for women in defined age groups, the use of the contraceptive pill, menopausal state and use of hormone replacement therapy.

There was also a short interview, using CAPI, conducted at the end of the seven dietary recording days (post-dietary record interview). Respondents were asked about any problems they experienced in keeping the diary, whether their consumption of specific foods had changed during the seven days and whether they had been unwell at all during the recording period. Respondents were also asked to complete an eating restraint questionnaire, using computer assisted self-interviewing (CASI) or on paper. Information was also collected on prescribed medications taken during the seven days.

The interview questionnaire is reproduced in Appendix A of the Technical Report[3].

1.3.2 The dietary record

The survey used a weighed intake methodology since its main aims were to provide detailed quantitative information on the range and distribution of intakes of foods and nutrients for respondents aged 19 to 64 years in Great Britain, and to investigate relationships between nutrient intakes, physical activity levels and various nutritional status and health measures. The advantages and disadvantages of this method and the factors affecting the choice are discussed in Appendix F of the Technical Report[3].

In deciding to use a weighed intake methodology, the period over which to collect information needed to be long enough to give reliable information on usual food consumption, balanced against the likelihood of poor compliance if the recording period was lengthy. The doubly labelled water study carried out as part of the feasibility study to assess the validity of the seven-day weighed intake method indicated a level of under-reporting that is typical of this method but no evidence of differential bias by age or sex. The feasibility study concluded that it was possible to collect dietary information for a seven-day period from respondents and that the quality of information would be acceptable (*see* Appendix C of the Technical Report[3]).

Information which would be of use to the interviewer when checking the dietary record was also collected: for example, on respondents' usual eating pattern on weekdays and at weekends; and on the types of certain common food items eaten, such as milk, bread and fat. This information was recorded on a paper form rather than in the CAPI program, so that the interviewer could use it to check diary entries during the recording period (*see* F7, Appendix A of the Technical Report[3]).

Respondents were asked to keep a weighed record of all food and drink they consumed, both in and out of the home, over seven consecutive days. Each respondent was issued with a set of accurately calibrated Soehnle Quanta digital food scales and two recording diaries; the 'Home Record' diary for use when it was possible for foods to be weighed, generally foods eaten in the home; and a smaller 'Eating and Drinking Away From Home' diary (the 'Eating Out' diary) for use when foods could not be weighed, generally foods eaten away from home. The respondent was also issued with a pocket-sized notebook for recording any of this information in circumstances where they were reluctant or it was inappropriate to carry the 'Eating Out' diary. The instruction and recording pages from these documents relating to the dietary information are included in Appendix A of the Technical Report[3].

The respondent, together with any other household member who might be involved in keeping the diary, for example their spouse or partner, was shown by the interviewer how to use the scales to weigh food and drinks, how to weigh and record leftovers, and how to record any food that was spilt or otherwise lost and so could not be re-weighed.

The 'Home Record' diary was the main recording and coding document. For each item consumed over the seven days a description of the item was recorded, including the brand name of the product and, where appropriate, the method of preparation. Also recorded was the weight served and the weight of any leftovers, the time food was eaten, whether it was eaten at home or elsewhere, and whether fruit and vegetables were home grown, defined as being grown in the household's own garden or allotment. The person who did the weighing, the respondent or someone else, was also recorded for each food item and, for each day, the respondent was asked to indicate whether they were 'well' or 'unwell'.

Respondents who completed a full seven-day dietary record were given a £10 gift voucher by the interviewer, as a token of appreciation. It was made clear that receiving the voucher was not dependent on co-operation with any other component of the survey, in particular, consenting to provide a blood sample.

Respondents started to record their consumption in the diaries as soon as the interviewer had explained the procedure and left the home, although the seven-day recording period started from midnight. The interviewer called back approximately 24 hours after placing the diaries in order to check that the items were being recorded correctly, to give encouragement and to re-motivate where appropriate. Everything consumed by the respondent had to be recorded, including medicines taken by mouth, vitamin and mineral supplements, and drinks of water. Respondents were encouraged to weigh everything they could, including takeaway meals brought into the home to eat. Where a served item could not be weighed, respondents were asked to record a description of the portion size, using standard household measures, or to describe the size of the item in some other way. Each separate item of food in a served portion needed to be weighed separately in order that the nutrient composition of each food item could be calculated. In addition, recipes for all home-made dishes were collected.

The amount of salt used either at the table or in cooking was not weighed, however questions on the use of salt in the cooking of the respondent's food and their use of salt at the table were asked at the dietary interview. All other sauces, pickles and dressings were recorded.

Vitamin and mineral supplements and artificial sweeteners were recorded as units consumed: for example, one Boots Vitamin C tablet 200mg, one teaspoon of Canderel Spoonful.

A large amount of detail needed to be recorded in the dietary record to enable similar foods prepared and cooked by different methods to be coded correctly, as such foods will have different nutrient compositions. Information could also be needed on cooking method, preparation and packaging as well as an exact description of the item before it could be accurately coded. Details on the recording of leftovers and spillage are given in Appendix F of the Technical Report[3]. An aide-memoire on using the scales and recording in the 'Home Diary' was left with respondents (see W1 and W2, Appendix A of the Technical Report[3]).

The 'Eating Out' diary was intended to be used only when it was not possible to weigh the food items. In such cases, respondents were asked to write down as much information as possible about each food item consumed, particularly the portion size and an estimate of the amount of any left over. Prices, descriptions, brand names, place of purchase, and the time and place where the food was consumed were all recorded. In certain circumstances, interviewers were allowed to purchase duplicate items which they would then weigh.

Where the respondent consumed food or drink items provided by their workplace or college, the interviewer was required to visit the workplace/college canteen to collect further information from the catering manager about, for example, cooking methods, portion sizes and types of fats used. The information was recorded on a 'catering questionnaire' which included standard questions on portion sizes and cooking methods, and had provision for recording information on specific items that the respondent had consumed (see Appendix A of the Technical Report[3]).

At each visit to the household, interviewers checked the diary entries with the respondent to ensure that they were complete and all the necessary detail had been recorded. Reasons for any apparent omission of meals were probed by the interviewers and noted on the diaries. If the interviewers probing uncovered food items that had been consumed but not recorded, these were added to the diary at the appropriate place. Before returning the coded diaries to ONS headquarters, interviewers were asked to make an assessment of the quality of the dietary record, in particular the extent to which they considered that the diary was an accurate reflection of the respondent's actual diet.

Interviewers were trained in and responsible for coding the food diaries so they could readily identify the level of detail needed for different food items and probe for missing detail at later visits to the household. A food code list, giving code numbers for about 3,500 items and a full description of each item, was prepared by nutritionists at the Food Standards Agency and the ONS, for use by the interviewers. As fieldwork progressed, further codes were added to the food code list for home-made recipe dishes and new products found in the dietary records. A page from the food code list is reproduced in Appendix A of the Technical Report[3].

Brand information was collected for all food items bought pre-wrapped, as some items, such as biscuits, confectionery and breakfast cereals, could not be food coded correctly unless the brand was known. Brand information was only coded for artificial sweeteners, bottled waters, herbal teas and herbal drinks, and soft drinks and fruit juices, to ensure adequate differentiation of these items. Food source codes were also allocated to each meal in order to identify food obtained and consumed outside the home. The contribution to total nutrient intake by foods from different sources could then be calculated.

After the interviewers had coded the entries in the dietary records, ONS headquarters coding and editing staff checked the documents. ONS nutritionists carried out initial checks for completeness of the dietary records, dealt with specific queries from interviewers and coding staff, and advised on and checked the quality of coding, with advice from Food Standards Agency nutritionists. They were also responsible for converting descriptions of portion sizes to weights, and checking that the appropriate codes for recipes and new products had been used. Computer checks for completeness and consistency of information were run on the dietary and questionnaire data. Following completion of these checks and calculations, the information from the dietary record was linked to the nutrient databank; nutrient intakes were thereby calculated from quantities of food consumed. This nutrient databank, which was compiled by the Food Standards Agency, holds information on 56 nutrients for each of 6,000 food codes. Further details of the nutrient databank are provided in Appendix H of the Technical Report[3]. Each food code used was also allocated to one of 115 subsidiary food groups; these were aggregated into 57 main food groups and further aggregated into 11 food types (see Appendix G of the Technical Report[3]).

1.4 Response and weighting

Table 1.1 shows response to the dietary interview and dietary record overall and by fieldwork wave[12]. Of the 5,673 addresses[13] (see Chapter 2 of the Technical Report[3]) issued to the interviewers, 35% were ineligible for the survey. This high rate of ineligibility is mainly due to the exclusion of those aged under 19 years and those aged 65 years or over. Just over one-third of the eligible sample, 37%, refused outright to take part in the survey. Only 2% of the eligible sample were not contacted. Overall, 61% of the eligible sample completed the dietary interview, including 47% who completed a full seven-day dietary record. Overall, 77% of those who completed the dietary interview completed a full seven-day dietary record.

While there has been a general fall in response to government social surveys over the last decade[14], the level of refusal to this NDNS was higher than expected. Steps were taken at an early stage to improve response, and included reissuing non-productive cases[15], developing the interviewer training to address further response issues, providing general guidance on approaching and explaining the survey to respondents, and increased support to the interviewers and their managers. This met with some success so that in Wave 4 a higher proportion of the eligible sample, 67%, completed the dietary interview compared with previous waves, 56% to 60%. Those who completed the dietary record had a similar demographic profile, by sex, age and social class of the Household Reference Person to those who completed the dietary interview (see also Chapter 2 of the Technical Report[3]).

The potential for bias in any dataset increases as the level of non-response increases. This is because there is an increased risk that little or no information will be collected on particular subgroups within the study population. An independent evaluation of the potential impact of non-response bias was undertaken by the University of Southampton[16]. The authors concluded that there was no evidence to suggest serious non-response bias, although this should be interpreted with caution as bias estimates were based upon assumptions about the total refusals and non-contacts for whom there was very little information. The authors recommended population-based weighting by sex, age and region. Indeed, without weighting for the differential response effect, estimates for different groups would be biased estimates because, in particular, they under-represent men and the youngest age group. To correct for this, the data presented in this volume and the other volumes of this survey have been weighted using a combined weight, based on differential sampling probabilities and differential non-response. Bases in tables are weighted bases scaled back to the number of cases in the responding and diary samples. Unweighted bases are given in Appendix B on page 90. Further details of the weighting procedures are given in Appendix D of the Technical Report[3].

In summary, the estimates presented in this report result from weighting the data as effectively as possible using the available information. However, results should be interpreted with caution, particularly where the sample sizes are low. The reader should note that the sample size in Scotland is particularly low and therefore standard errors may be large (*see* Appendix A, pages 83-86, for further details on standard errors).

(Table 1.1)

References and endnotes

[1] The other volumes in this series are:

   (i)   Types and quantities of foods consumed, published December 2002;

   (ii)   Micronutrient intakes (vitamins and minerals, including urinary analytes), to be published in summer 2003;

   (iii) Nutritional status (blood pressure, anthropometry, blood analytes and physical activity), to be published in autumn 2003;

   (iv) Summary report, providing a summary of the key findings from the four volumes, to be published in autumn 2003.

[2] Gregory J, Foster K, Tyler H, Wiseman M. *The Dietary and Nutritional Survey of British Adults.* HMSO (London, 1990).

[3] The Technical Report is available online at http://www.food.gov.uk/science.

[4] For further information about the archived data contact:

   The Data Archive
   University of Essex
   Wivenhoe Park
   Colchester
   Essex CO4 3SQ
   United Kingdom
   Tel: (UK) 01206 872001
   Fax: (UK) 01206 872003
   E-mail: archive@essex.ac.uk
   Website: www.data-archive.ac.uk

[5] Responsibility for this survey and the National Diet and Nutrition Survey programme transferred from the Ministry of Agriculture, Fisheries and Food to the Food Standards Agency on its establishment in April 2000.

[6] Finch S, Doyle W, Lowe C, Bates CJ, Prentice A, Smithers G, Clarke PC. *National Diet and Nutrition Survey: people aged 65 years and over. Volume 1: Report of the diet and nutrition survey.* TSO (London, 1998).

[7] Gregory JR, Collins DL, Davies PSW, Hughes JM, Clarke PC. *National Diet and Nutrition Survey: children aged 1½ to 4½ years. Volume 1: Report of the diet and nutrition survey.* HMSO (London, 1995).

[8] Gregory JR, Lowe S, Bates CJ, Prentice A, Jackson LV, Smithers G, Wenlock R, Farron M. *National Diet and Nutrition Survey: young people aged 4 to 18 years. Volume 1: Report of the diet and nutrition survey.* TSO (London, 2000).

[9] Initially 30 addresses were selected within each postal sector. Results from Wave 1 indicated a higher level of age-related ineligibles than expected and a much lower response rate. In order to increase the actual number of diaries completed and to give interviewers enough work an extra 10 addresses were selected for Waves 2, 3 and 4.

[10] The diet and physiology of pregnant or breastfeeding women is likely to be so different from those of other similarly aged women as possibly to distort the results. Further, as the number of pregnant or breastfeeding women identified within the overall sample of 2000 would not be adequate for analysis as a single group, it was decided that they should be regarded as ineligible for interview.

[11] Selecting only one eligible adult per household reduces the burden of the survey on the household and therefore reduces possible detrimental effects on co-operation and data quality. It also reduces the clustering of the sample associated with similar dietary behaviour within the same household and improves the precision of the estimates.

[12] As in some cases fieldwork extended beyond the end of the three-month fieldwork wave, or cases were re-allocated to another fieldwork wave, cases have been allocated to a wave for analysis purposes as follows. Any case started more than four weeks after the end of the official fieldwork wave has been allocated to the actual quarter in which it started. For example, all cases allocated to Wave 1 and started July to October 2000 appear as Wave 1 cases. Any case allocated to Wave 1 and started in November 2000 or later appears in a subsequent wave; for example a case allocated to Wave 1 which started in November 2000 is counted as Wave 2. All cases in Wave 4 (April to June 2001) had been started by the end of July 2001.

[13] Initially 1,140 addresses were issued per wave. This was increased in Wave 2 to 1,520 addresses, 40 in each quota of work. In Wave 3, 27 addresses were withdrawn. These were unapproachable due to access restrictions in place because of the foot-and-mouth disease outbreak.

[14] Martin J and Matheson J Responses to declining response rates on government surveys. *Survey Methodology Bulletin* 1999; **45**: 33–37.

[15] Non-productive cases are those where the interviewer was unable to make contact with the selected household or respondent (non-contacts) and where the household or selected respondent refused to take part in the survey (refusals). Addresses that were returned to the office coded as refusals or non-contacts were considered for reissue. Where it was thought that a non-productive case might result in at least a dietary interview (for example, where the selected respondent had said they were too busy at the time of the original call but would be available at a later date) these addresses were issued to interviewers working in subsequent waves of fieldwork.

[16] Skinner CJ and Holmes D (2001) *The 2000–01 National Diet and Nutrition Survey of Adults Aged 19–64 years: The Impact of Non-response.* University of Southampton. Reproduced as Appendix E of the Technical Report (*see* note 3).

Table 1.1

Response to the dietary interview and seven-day dietary record by wave of fieldwork*

Unweighted data   Numbers and percentages

| | Wave of fieldwork | | | | | | | | All | |
| | Wave 1: July–September | | Wave 2: October–December | | Wave 3: January–March | | Wave 4: April–June | | | |
	No.	%	No.	%	No.	%	No.	%	No.	%
Set sample = 100%	1098	100	1397	100	1450	100	1728	100	5673	100
Ineligible	382	35	514	37	515	36	558	32	1969	35
Eligible sample = 100%	716	100	883	100	935	100	1170	100	3704	100
Non-contacts	12	2	24	3	23	2	30	3	89	2
Refusals	271	38	369	42	364	39	360	31	1364	37
Co-operation with:										
dietary interview	433	60	490	56	548	59	780	67	2251	61
seven-day dietary record	325	45	385	44	429	46	585	50	1724	47

Note: * For productive cases, fieldwork wave is defined as the wave (quarter) in which the dietary interview took place; for unproductive cases, fieldwork wave is the wave in which the case
       was issued (or reissued).

2 Energy intake

2.1 Introduction

In this and the following three chapters, data are presented on the intakes of energy and macronutrients by respondents in the survey who kept a dietary record for the full seven days, a total of 1,724 respondents. Intakes of energy and macronutrients are presented separately for men and women in four age groups, 19 to 24 years, 25 to 34 years, 35 to 49 years, and 50 to 64 years. Variation in intake of energy and macronutrients according to the main socio-demographic characteristics of the respondents is also discussed, and for energy and selected nutrients the percentage of the total intake derived from different food types is shown.

Intake data are presented as average daily amounts, that is the seven-day intake derived from the dietary record averaged to produce a daily intake. For energy and each nutrient the mean and standard deviation of the intakes are given, together with selected points in the cumulative distribution, the 2.5th, 50th (median) and 97.5th percentiles. Where appropriate, intakes for groups of respondents are compared with the Dietary Reference Values (DRVs) as defined by the Department of Health in the report *Dietary Reference Values for Food Energy and Nutrients for the United Kingdom* [1].

Tables in this chapter present data on total energy (including energy from alcohol), except for Tables 2.2 and 2.4 which present data on intake of food energy (which excludes energy from alcohol). The majority of tables show energy intake expressed as megajoules (MJ), key tables and textual figures also give kilocalorie values (kcal) [2].

2.2 Intake of energy

Tables 2.1 and 2.3 show average daily total energy intake for men and women in MJ and kcal respectively. The mean daily total energy intake for men was 9.72MJ (2313kcal) and for women, 6.87MJ (1632kcal) (ns). There were no statistically significant differences in the mean daily total energy intake by age for men or women.

In general, mean daily total energy intake values were close to or the same as the median values. For example, for men aged 50 to 64 years the mean and median daily total energy intakes were 9.55MJ. However, there was a wide range of intakes in each age and sex group. For example, for those aged 19 to 24 years, intakes at the lower 2.5 percentile were 5.53MJ (1315kcal) for men, and 3.21MJ (761kcal) for women, while at the upper 2.5 percentile intakes were 15.19MJ (3611kcal) and 10.36MJ (2460kcal) for men and women respectively. In the oldest group for men, 50 to 64 years, intakes at the lower and upper 2.5 percentiles were 4.69MJ and 14.33MJ (1110kcal and 3409kcal) respectively.

Tables 2.2 and 2.4 show average daily food energy intake (that is excluding energy from alcohol) for men and women in MJ and kcal respectively. The mean daily food energy intake for men was 8.88MJ (2110kcal) and for women, 6.54MJ (1554kcal) (ns). There were no statistically significant differences in mean daily food energy intake by age for men or women.

(Tables 2.1 to 2.4)

2.2.1 Energy intake and Estimated Average Requirements

Estimates of energy requirements of different population groups are termed 'Estimated Average Requirements' (EARs) and are defined as the energy intake estimated to meet the *average* requirements of the population group. EARs were set by the Committee on Medical Aspects of Food Policy (COMA) and were based largely on energy expenditure data[1].

Table 2.5 shows actual energy intake as a percentage of the appropriate EAR for the eight sex and age groups in the survey. Actual intake as a percentage of the appropriate EAR was calculated for each respondent and the mean percentages are shown in the table.

Mean daily total energy intakes were below EARs for each sex and age group and ranged from 82% of the EAR for women aged 25 to 34 years to 94% of the EAR for men aged 35 to 49 years. In general, the mean energy intake for men was closer to the EAR than for women. For example, men aged 25 to 34 years had a mean energy intake of 9.82MJ (2337kcal) which is 93% of the EAR. In comparison, women aged 25 to 34 had a mean energy intake of 6.61MJ (1570 kcal) 82% of the EAR. For all sex and age groups mean energy intakes were significantly lower than the EAR for that group.

Mean energy intakes below EARs have been found for other populations surveyed in the NDNS programme, all of which have used the same dietary methodology. For example in the survey of young people, among those aged 15 to 18 years mean energy intake was 83% of the EAR for boys and 77% for girls. In the survey of people aged 65 years and over, the mean energy intakes for free living men and women were 85% and 76% respectively of the EAR. As was noted in the reports of these previous surveys, the difference between estimated intakes and EARs could arise from an inadequate energy intake, a biased low estimate of intake due to respondents mis-reporting their actual intake or modifying their diet during the recording period, or an overestimate of energy requirements[3,4].

In the feasibility study for this survey, estimates of energy intake using the seven-day weighed dietary record methodology were compared with measurements of energy expenditure using the doubly labelled water (DLW) methodology[5,6]. The data showed that the estimates of energy intake for both sexes and most age groups were below both the EARs and total energy expenditure as measured using the DLW. However there was no evidence of differential bias by age or sex. Overall, the agreement between the estimates for energy expenditure derived from the doubly labelled water analysis and energy intake derived from the dietary record indicated a degree of

under-reporting typical of this particular methodology for assessing energy intake. This was in the region of a 25% under-estimation of energy intake on average. Particular attention was paid in the mainstage survey to improving the quality of the dietary information by probing and checking. However, it remains likely that the estimates of energy intake are underestimates. No attempt has been made to adjust the energy and nutrient intakes presented in this report to take account of under-reporting.

(Table 2.5)

2.3   Variation in total energy intake

Caveat
This section looks at the variation in mean daily total energy intake by the main classificatory variables. Inter-relationships between the main classificatory variables need to be borne in mind when interpreting these results. For example, there is significant variation in the age distribution of respondents by household composition, household benefit status and economic activity status and any variation associated with these characteristics may be partly accounted for by variation by age (or equally variation with age could be accounted for by variation with other characteristics)[7].

2.3.1   Region

Table 2.6 shows the mean daily total energy intake for men and women by region[8]. There were no statistically significant differences in mean energy intake between regions.

(Table 2.6)

2.3.2   Household Composition

Table 2.7 shows the mean daily total energy intake of respondents by household composition. There were few significant differences in mean energy intake by differences in household composition. Women living with a spouse/partner and no dependent children had a significantly higher mean energy intake, 7.09MJ (1694kcal), than those living with dependent children but no spouse/partner, 6.13MJ (1465kcal) (p<0.01). However, it should be noted that the difference might be associated in part with the age structure of the different household compositions[7].

(Table 2.7)

2.3.3   Household receipt of benefits

Table 2.8 shows that for both men and women mean daily total energy intake was significantly lower for those living in households where someone was in receipt of benefits than for those in non-benefit households[9]. For example, in benefit households mean daily energy intake was 8.85MJ (2115kcal) for men and 6.37MJ (1522kcal) for women compared with 9.86MJ (2357kcal) for men and 6.97 MJ (1666kcal) for women in non-benefit households (p<0.05).

(Table 2.8)

2.3.4 Economic activity status

Economic activity status categorises unemployed and working respondents as economically active and others, for example, those who are retired and those who are at home looking after children, as economically inactive[10].

Table 2.9 shows that for both sexes those who were economically active had a significantly higher mean daily total energy intake than those who were economically inactive. For example, men who were economically active had a mean daily energy intake of 9.88MJ (2361kcal) compared with 8.61MJ (2058kcal) for those who were economically inactive (p<0.01). For women these figures were 6.98MJ (1668kcal) and 6.55MJ (1565kcal) respectively (p<0.01). However, it should be noted that these differences might be associated in part with differences in the age structure of those who are economically active compared with those who are economically inactive[7].

(Table 2.9)

2.4. Contribution of main food types to intake of energy

Table 2.10 shows the percentage contribution of the major food types to the mean daily total energy intake for respondents by sex and age. There were no significant sex or age differences in the contributions of the different food groups to energy intake.

The main contributor to energy intake was cereals & cereal products, providing about one third of the mean energy intake (31%). Within this group, bread accounted for 13% of energy intake.

Meat & meat products contributed 15% to energy intake, and milk & milk products a further 10%, half of which came from liquid milk.

Drinks, including alcoholic drinks, contributed 10% to average daily energy intake; this was mainly in the form of alcoholic drinks.

Potatoes & savoury snacks accounted for a further 9% of energy intake. The main contributor within this food group was chips, which provided 4% of

energy intake. Sugar, preserves & confectionery provided 6% of energy intake, mainly from table sugar and chocolate confectionery.

(Table 2.10)

References and endnotes

[1] Department of Health. Report on Health and Social Subjects: 41. *Dietary Reference Values for Food Energy and Nutrients for the United Kingdom*. HMSO (London, 1991).

[2] Calculated values quoted in the text are based on a conversion factor of 1kcal = 4.184 kJ. Tables 2.3 and 2.4 shows average daily energy intake in kcals produced from analysis of the dataset. The small differences between these kcal values and equivalent values calculated using the conversion factor are due to rounding.

[3] Gregory J, Lowe S, Bates CJ, Prentice A, Jackson LV, Smithers G, Wenlock R, Farron M. *National Diet and Nutrition Survey: young people aged 4 to 18 years. Volume 1: Report of the diet and nutrition survey.* TSO (London, 2000).

[4] Finch S, Doyle W, Lowe C, Bates CJ, Prentice A, Smithers G, Clarke PC. *National Diet and Nutrition Survey: people aged 65 years and over. Volume 1: Report of the diet and nutrition survey.* TSO (London, 1998).

[5] The feasibility study report is reproduced as Appendix C of the Technical Report, which can be found at http://www.food.gov.uk/science.

[6] Coward WA, Wright A, Bluck LJC. *Comparisons between energy intake and energy expenditure in the NDNS survey, adults aged 19–64 years.* MRC Resource Centre for Human Nutrition Research (Cambridge, 2000). Paper produced from feasibility study data for NDNS Steering Committee.

[7] Chapter 2 of the Technical Report includes information on inter-relationships between the main socio-economic variables and gives tables of distributions for household composition, household benefit status and economic activity status by sex and age of respondent - Tables 2.18 , 2.23 and 2.20 respectively. The Technical Report is available online at http://www.food.gov.uk/science.

[8] The areas included in each of the four analysis 'regions' are given in the response chapter, Chapter 2 of the Technical Report, online at http://www.food.gov.uk/science. Definitions of 'regions' are given in the glossary (*see* Appendix C).

[9] Households receiving benefits are those where someone in the respondent's household was currently receiving Working Families Tax Credit or had, in the previous 14 days, drawn Income Support or (Income-related) Job Seeker's Allowance. Definitions of 'household' and 'benefits (receiving)' are given in the glossary (*see* Appendix C).

[10] The small number of respondents classified as unemployed would make it impossible to check reliably for significant differences between, for example, estimates of nutrient intake by employment status. It was decided therefore to use economic activity as a more appropriate indicator. This categorises unemployed and working respondents as economically active and others as economically inactive. (*See also* Chapter 2 of the Technical Report.)

Table 2.1

Average daily total energy intake (MJ) by sex and age of respondent

Cumulative percentages

Energy intake (MJ)	Age (years):				All
	19–24	25–34	35–49	50–64	
	cum %	cum %	cum %	cum %	cum %
Men					
Less than 5.00	1	0	2	4	2
Less than 6.00	6	3	6	7	5
Less than 7.00	13	11	12	12	12
Less than 8.00	19	24	22	25	23
Less than 9.00	49	41	35	43	40
Less than 10.00	66	58	52	59	57
Less than 11.00	76	72	71	74	73
Less than 12.00	92	86	83	85	85
Less than 13.00	94	91	92	90	91
All	100	100	100	100	100
Base	*108*	*219*	*253*	*253*	*833*
Mean (average value)	9.44	9.82	9.93	9.55	9.72
Median	9.00	9.66	9.89	9.55	9.62
Lower 2.5 percentile	5.53	5.94	5.50	4.69	5.50
Upper 2.5 percentile	15.19	16.75	15.52	14.33	14.86
Standard deviation	2.198	2.465	2.581	2.381	2.446
	cum %	cum %	cum %	cum %	cum %
Women					
Less than 2.00	-	-	0	0	0
Less than 3.00	-	1	2	2	1
Less than 4.00	10	6	4	3	5
Less than 5.00	15	18	12	11	13
Less than 6.00	26	33	28	30	29
Less than 7.00	50	60	48	53	53
Less than 8.00	67	78	74	74	74
Less than 9.00	86	93	88	89	89
Less than 10.00	96	98	96	96	96
All	100	100	100	100	100
Base	*104*	*210*	*318*	*259*	*891*
Mean (average value)	7.00	6.61	6.96	6.91	6.87
Median	6.97	6.71	7.09	6.76	6.88
Lower 2.5 percentile	3.21	3.36	3.15	3.12	3.28
Upper 2.5 percentile	10.36	9.87	10.73	10.54	10.48
Standard deviation	1.925	1.636	1.780	1.746	1.758

Table 2.2

Average daily food energy* intake (MJ) by sex and age of respondent

Cumulative percentages

Energy intake (MJ)	Age (years):				All
	19–24	25–34	35–49	50–64	
	cum %	cum %	cum %	cum %	cum%
Men					
Less than 5.00	3	2	4	5	4
Less than 6.00	11	8	9	11	10
Less than 7.00	23	21	19	22	21
Less than 8.00	31	37	31	35	34
Less than 9.00	61	57	49	55	55
Less than 10.00	80	73	68	75	73
Less than 11.00	88	85	83	85	85
Less than 12.00	96	92	91	92	92
Less than 13.00	97	95	94	94	95
All	100	100	100	100	100
Base	*108*	*219*	*253*	*253*	*833*
Mean (average value)	8.61	8.94	9.05	8.76	8.88
Median	8.62	8.56	9.03	8.72	8.72
Lower 2.5 percentile	4.65	5.00	4.64	4.54	4.69
Upper 2.5 percentile	13.20	14.86	14.70	13.47	14.14
Standard deviation	2.096	2.444	2.514	2.322	2.388
	cum %	cum%	cum%	cum%	cum%
Women					
Less than 4.00	11	8	7	5	7
Less than 5.00	17	22	17	16	18
Less than 6.00	40	42	35	39	38
Less than 7.00	61	71	56	59	61
Less than 8.00	80	86	80	79	81
Less than 9.00	90	97	92	92	93
Less than 10.00	97	99	96	97	97
All	100	100	100	100	100
Base	*104*	*210*	*318*	*259*	*891*
Mean (average value)	6.56	6.27	6.64	6.63	6.54
Median	6.54	6.35	6.68	6.52	6.52
Lower 2.5 percentile	3.18	3.25	3.07	3.11	3.15
Upper 2.5 percentile	10.04	9.56	10.32	10.51	10.12
Standard deviation	1.858	1.588	1.773	1.720	1.730

*Note: * Food energy excludes energy from alcohol.*

Table 2.3

Average daily total energy intake (kcal) by sex and age of respondent

Cumulative percentages

Energy intake (kcal)	Age (years):				All
	19–24	25–34	35–49	50–64	
	cum %	cum %	cum %	cum %	cum %
Men					
Less than 1000	1	0	1	1	1
Less than 1500	8	7	8	9	8
Less than 1750	18	15	15	16	16
Less than 2000	26	27	25	32	28
Less than 2250	58	47	43	50	48
Less than 2500	70	65	59	69	65
Less than 2750	85	81	78	81	81
Less than 3000	94	90	89	88	90
All	100	100	100	100	100
Base	*108*	*219*	*253*	*253*	*833*
Mean (average value)	2247	2337	2361	2271	2313
Median	2146	2294	2349	2263	2287
Lower 2.5 percentile	1315	1413	1302	1110	1302
Upper 2.5 percentile	3611	3987	3699	3409	3528
Standard deviation	525	587	614	567	582
	cum %	cum %	cum %	cum %	cum %
Women					
Less than 800	3	2	3	3	3
Less than 1000	12	6	5	5	6
Less than 1200	15	17	12	12	14
Less than 1400	25	32	26	27	27
Less than 1600	44	51	44	49	47
Less than 1800	61	70	63	65	65
Less than 2000	78	87	83	81	83
Less than 2250	90	96	92	94	93
All	100	100	100	100	100
Base	*104*	*210*	*318*	*259*	*891*
Mean (average value)	1665	1570	1654	1642	1632
Median	1654	1594	1681	1607	1633
Lower 2.5 percentile	761	797	747	738	781
Upper 2.5 percentile	2460	2347	2554	2506	2494
Standard deviation	459	390	424	415	418

Table 2.4

Average daily food energy* intake (kcal) by sex and age of respondent

Cumulative percentages

Energy intake (kcal)	Age (years):				All
	19–24	25–34	35–49	50–64	
	cum %	cum %	cum %	cum %	cum%
Men					
Less than 1000	2	1	2	1	1
Less than 1500	17	14	14	13	14
Less than 1750	28	24	23	27	25
Less than 2000	42	45	40	45	43
Less than 2250	71	66	59	64	64
Less than 2500	84	79	78	82	80
Less than 2750	90	89	87	88	88
Less than 3000	97	94	94	93	94
All	100	100	100	100	100
Base	*108*	*219*	*253*	*253*	*833*
Mean (average value)	2047	2125	2151	2083	2110
Median	2051	2033	2145	2075	2072
Lower 2.5 percentile	1107	1189	1104	1083	1112
Upper 2.5 percentile	3148	3528	3490	3208	3348
Standard deviation	500	581	597	552	568
	cum%	cum%	cum%	cum%	cum%
Women					
Less than 800	4	3	3	3	3
Less than 1000	13	10	8	6	8
Less than 1500	44	49	42	45	45
Less than 1750	69	75	68	68	70
Less than 2000	85	90	86	86	87
Less than 2250	92	97	94	96	95
Less than 2500	99	100	98	98	99
All	100		100	100	100
Base	*104*	*210*	*318*	*259*	*891*
Mean (average value)	1559	1490	1577	1574	1554
Median	1557	1511	1586	1542	1550
Lower 2.5 percentile	752	775	733	738	747
Upper 2.5 percentile	2384	2278	2458	2497	2404
Standard deviation	442	378	422	409	411

*Note: * Food energy excludes energy from alcohol.*

Table 2.5

Average daily total energy intake (MJ) as a percentage of the estimated average requirement (EAR) by sex and age of respondent*

Sex and age of respondent	Mean energy intake (MJ)	Intake as % EAR**	Base
Men aged (years):			
19–24	9.44	89	108
25–34	9.82	93	219
35–49	9.93	94	253
50–64	9.55	92	253
All	9.72	92	833
Women aged (years):			
19–24	7.00	86	104
25–34	6.61	82	210
35–49	6.96	86	318
50–64	6.91	87	259
All	6.87	85	891

Note: * Department of Health. Report on Health and Social Subjects: 41. Dietary Reference Values for Food Energy and Nutrients for the United Kingdom. HMSO (London, 1991).

** The Estimated Average Requirements (EARs) for energy are:

Men: 19 to 50 years: 10.60MJ/d	Women:19 to 50 years: 8.10MJ/d
51 to 59 years: 10.60MJ/d	51 to 59 years: 8.00MJ/d
60 to 64 years: 9.93MJ/d	60 to 64 years: 7.99MJ/d

Energy intake as a percentage of EAR was calculated for each respondent using the EAR appropriate for sex and age.

Table 2.6

Average daily intake of total energy (MJ) by sex of respondent and region

Energy intake (MJ)	Region				All
	Scotland	Northern	Central, South West and Wales	London and the South East	
Men					
Mean (average value)	9.81	9.45	9.99	9.64	9.72
Median	9.82	9.43	9.80	9.65	9.62
Standard deviation	2.52	2.23	2.66	2.33	2.45
Base	65	234	294	240	833
Women					
Mean (average value)	6.73	6.77	6.90	6.94	6.87
Median	6.40	6.61	6.96	6.95	6.88
Standard deviation	1.52	1.84	1.67	1.85	1.76
Base	66	229	327	268	891

Table 2.7

Average daily intake of total energy (MJ) by sex of respondent and household composition

Household composition	Energy intake (MJ)			
	Mean	Median	sd	Base
Men				
Living alone	9.50	9.67	2.73	100
Living with others, no dependent children				
with spouse/partner	9.86	9.68	2.43	333
with other adults, no spouse/partner	9.56	9.13	2.33	146
Living with dependent children with or				
without spouse or partner*	9.72	9.72	2.42	254
All	9.72	9.62	2.45	833
Women				
Living alone	6.88	6.81	2.07	94
Living with others, no dependent children				
with spouse/partner	7.09	7.12	1.65	364
with other adults, no spouse/partner	6.84	6.88	1.60	100
Living with dependent children				
with spouse/partner	6.76	6.75	1.74	260
without spouse/partner	6.13	6.03	1.95	72
All	6.87	6.88	1.76	891

Note: * Due to the small numbers in the sample, men living with dependent children without spouse or partner are not reported separately .

Table 2.8

Average daily intake of total energy (MJ) by sex of respondent and whether someone in respondent's household was receiving certain benefits

Energy intake (MJ)	Whether benefits received		All
	Receiving benefits	Not receiving benefits	
Men			
Mean (average value)	8.85	9.86	9.72
Median	9.00	9.75	9.62
Standard deviation	2.514	2.409	2.446
Base	110	723	833
Women			
Mean (average value)	6.37	6.97	6.87
Median	6.24	6.97	6.88
Standard deviation	2.091	1.667	1.758
Base	150	741	891

Table 2.9

Average daily intake of total energy (MJ) by sex of respondent and economic activity status*

Energy intake (MJ)	Economic status		All
	Economically active	Economically inactive	
Men			
Mean (average value)	9.88	8.61	9.72
Median	9.81	8.65	9.62
Standard deviation	2.44	2.17	2.45
Base	731	102	833
Women			
Mean (average value)	6.98	6.55	6.87
Median	7.04	6.41	6.88
Standard deviation	1.71	1.84	1.76
Base	648	242	891

Note: * Economic activity status categorises respondents by whether they are economically active, that is in employment or actively
seeking work, or economically inactive, which includes those who are retired or at home looking after children.

Table 2.10

Percentage contribution of food types to average daily total energy intake (MJ) by sex and age of respondent

Percentages

Type of food	Men aged (years):				All men	Women aged (years):				All women	All
	19–24	25–34	35–49	50–64		19–24	25–34	35–49	50–64		
	%	%	%	%	%	%	%	%	%	%	%
Cereals & cereal products	27	30	30	31	30	28	32	31	31	31	31
of which:											
bread (white, wholemeal, soft grain, other)	11	13	13	14	13	13	13	12	12	12	13
breakfast cereals	2	4	4	5	4	4	4	5	6	5	3
biscuits	2	3	3	3	3	2	2	3	3	3	3
buns, cakes & pastries	2	2	3	4	3	1	4	4	5	4	3
Milk & milk products	6	9	10	10	9	9	11	11	12	11	10
of which:											
milk (whole, semi–skimmed, skimmed)	3	5	5	5	5	5	5	6	6	6	5
cheese (incl. cottage cheese)	2	3	3	3	3	3	3	3	3	3	3
Eggs & egg dishes	2	2	2	2	2	2	2	2	2	2	2
Fat spreads	4	3	4	5	4	3	3	4	4	4	4
Meat & meat products	19	17	17	15	17	16	13	14	13	14	15
of which:											
bacon & ham	2	2	2	2	2	1	1	1	1	1	1
beef, veal & dishes	3	3	3	3	3	3	2	3	3	3	3
lamb & dishes	1	1	1	1	1	0	0	1	1	1	1
pork & dishes	0	1	1	1	1	1	1	1	1	1	1
coated chicken	1	1	1	0	1	2	1	1	1	1	1
chicken, turkey & dishes	3	4	4	3	3	4	4	4	3	3	3
burgers & kebabs	3	2	1	0	1	2	1	1	0	1	1
sausages	2	2	2	1	2	1	1	1	1	1	1
meat pies & pastries	3	3	2	3	3	2	1	2	2	2	2
Fish & fish dishes	1	2	2	3	2	2	2	3	4	3	3
of which:											
coated &/or fried white fish	1	1	1	1	1	1	1	1	1	1	1
oily fish	0	1	1	1	1	1	1	1	2	1	1
Vegetables (excluding potatoes)	3	3	4	4	4	3	6	5	4	5	4
Potatoes & savoury snacks	12	9	9	9	9	14	11	9	8	10	9
of which:											
chips	6	4	4	3	4	6	4	3	3	4	4
other fried/roast potatoes & products	1	1	1	1	1	1	1	1	1	2	1
other potatoes & potato dishes	2	2	2	3	2	3	3	3	3	3	3
Fruit & nuts	1	2	3	4	3	2	3	3	4	3	2
Sugar, preserves & confectionery	6	6	6	5	6	5	6	6	5	5	6
of which:											
table sugar	2	3	3	3	3	1	2	2	2	2	2
chocolate confectionery	3	2	2	1	2	3	3	3	2	3	2
Drinks*	16	13	12	10	12	13	9	8	7	8	10
of which:											
fruit juice	1	1	1	1	1	1	1	1	1	1	1
soft drinks, not low calorie (concentrated, carbonated, ready to drink)	6	3	1	1	2	5	2	1	1	2	2
alcoholic drinks	9	9	9	8	9	6	5	5	4	5	7
Miscellaneous**	2	3	2	3	3	3	3	3	3	3	3
Average daily total energy intake (MJ)	**9.44**	**9.82**	**9.93**	**9.55**	**9.72**	**7.00**	**6.61**	**6.96**	**6.91**	**6.87**	**8.38**
Total number of respondents	**108**	**219**	**253**	**253**	**833**	**104**	**210**	**318**	**259**	**891**	**1724**

Note: * Includes soft drinks, alcoholic drinks, tea, coffee and water.

** Includes powdered beverages (except tea and coffee), soups, sauces, condiments and artificial sweeteners.

3 Protein and carbohydrate intake

3.1 Introduction

In this chapter, data are presented on intakes of protein and carbohydrates, the percentage of food energy provided by each, and the percentage contribution of food types to intakes of these nutrients. For carbohydrate, information is shown separately for total carbohydrate, non-milk extrinsic sugars, intrinsic and milk sugars (and starch), and non-starch polysaccharides ('fibre')[1].

3.2 Protein

Mean daily protein intake for men was 88.2g, significantly higher than that for women, 63.7g (p<0.01). Men aged 19 to 24 years and women aged 19 to 35 years had significantly lower mean daily intakes of protein than those aged 50 to 64 years (women aged 19 to 24 years: p<0.05; all others: p<0.01). For example, men and women aged 19 to 24 years had mean intakes of 77.8g and 59.9g respectively compared with 88.8g for men and 67.4g for women aged 50 to 64 years. In addition, men aged 19 to 24 years and women aged 25 to 34 years had significantly lower mean daily intakes of protein than those aged 35 to 49 years (p<0.01).

Generally within each age and sex group medians were close to the mean values and the range of intakes was large. For men aged 25 to 34 years, intake at the upper 2.5 percentile was very high, 156.2g. This was due to a small number of men in this age group who had consumed large quantities of food items containing a lot of protein, for example, milk & milk products and meat & meat products.

(Table 3.1)

As Table 3.2 shows, average protein intakes for all sex and age groups were well in excess of the UK Reference Nutrient Intake (RNI) for protein[2]. For each sex and age group, mean daily intake was at least 130% of the RNI.

(Table 3.2)

As shown in Table 3.3, protein provided on average 16.5% of the food energy for men and 16.6% for women in the survey (ns). Overall, men and women obtained a similar proportion of their food energy from protein, and this was true within each age group. Among men the youngest age group derived a significantly lower proportion of their food energy from protein than those in any other age group. For example, men aged 19 to 24 years derived 14.9% of their food energy from protein compared with 17.0% for those aged 50 to 64 years (p<0.01). Among women, the two youngest age groups derived a significantly lower proportion of their food energy from protein than the oldest group. For example, women aged 19 to 24 years derived 15.4% of their food energy from protein and those aged 25 to 34 years 15.9%, compared with 17.4% for women aged 50 to 64 years (p<0.01).

(Table 3.3)

Table 3.4 shows that around three-quarters of the protein consumed was derived from three main food types. Meat & meat products was the major source of protein, providing on average 36% of the daily intake overall, of which over a third came from coated chicken and chicken & turkey dishes. Cereals & cereal products provided 23% of the protein intake, of which about half came from bread. Milk & milk products provided a further 16% of the protein intake overall. There were no significant differences between men and women or by age in the proportion of protein intake obtained from different food types.

(Table 3.4)

3.3 Total carbohydrate

The mean daily intake of total carbohydrate was 275g for men and 203g for women (p<0.01). Mean intake for men was significantly higher than for women for all age groups apart from 19 to 24 year olds (p<0.01). There were no statistically significant differences in mean intake of total carbohydrate by age for men or women.

Within each age and sex group medians were close to the mean values and the range of intakes was large. For example, for men aged 35 to 49 years, intake at the lower 2.5 percentile was 130g compared with 494g at the upper 2.5 percentile.

(Table 3.5)

As shown in Table 3.6 total carbohydrate provided on average 47.7% of food energy intake for men and 48.5% for women (ns). There were no significant age differences for men or women in the proportion of food energy derived from total carbohydrate. At the lower 2.5 percentile, respondents derived just over one third of their food energy from total carbohydrate. At the upper 2.5 percentile close to 60% of food energy was derived from this source, with little variation by age or sex.

(Table 3.6)

Table 3.7 shows the main sources of total carbohydrate in the diets of respondents to this survey. Cereals & cereal products were the major source, contributing 45% to total carbohydrate intake overall. Within this group, bread contributed 21% and breakfast cereals 7%. Potatoes & savoury snacks provided 12% overall, of which 4% came from chips and 5% from 'other' potatoes, which includes boiled, mashed and baked potatoes. Drinks contributed a further 10%, mainly from carbonated soft drinks, not low calorie, and additionally for men, from beer & lager. Sugar, preserves & confectionery contributed 9% to intake, of which table sugar accounted for over half. The main sources did not vary significantly by age or sex.

(Table 3.7)

3.3.1 Sugars

Information is given on intakes of *non-milk extrinsic sugars* and *intrinsic and milk* sugars. This distinction is made on the basis of cariogenicity. Non-milk extrinsic sugars are considered to be a major contributor to the development of dental caries[2]. Relationships between the oral health of respondents and their intakes of sugars are not discussed in this report.

Extrinsic sugars are any sugars that are not contained within the cellular structure of the food, whether natural and unprocessed or refined. Examples are the sugars in honey, table sugar and lactose in milk and milk products. Non-milk extrinsic sugars are therefore all extrinsic sugars *excluding* lactose in milk and milk products, which is seen to be a special case as milk sugars are not cariogenic[2]. Intrinsic sugars are those contained within the cellular structure of the food; the category *intrinsic and milk sugars* includes intrinsic sugars plus lactose in milk and milk products.

The UK Dietary Reference Value for non-milk extrinsic sugars is 10% of total dietary energy or 11% of food energy, expressed as a population average[2]. It is recommended that starch and intrinsic and milk sugars should provide the balance of energy not provided by alcohol, protein, fat and non-milk extrinsic sugars, that is on average 37% of total dietary energy or 39% of food energy for the population. For comparative purposes, information on the percentage of food energy is shown for intrinsic and milk sugars and starch combined.

Non-milk extrinsic sugars

The mean daily intake of non-milk extrinsic sugars was 79g (median 71g) for men and 51g (median 44g) for women (p<0.01). Mean intake was significantly higher for men than for women for all age groups (all: p<0.01). Overall, mean intake was significantly higher for men aged 19 to 24 years, 96g, than for those aged 35 to 49 years, 78g, and those aged 50 to 64 years, 70g (35 to 49 years: p<0.05; 50 to 64 years: p<0.01). There were no significant differences by age for women.

Generally, within each age and sex group, there was a large difference between median and mean values[3]. This indicates that there were a small number of cases within each group with relatively large intakes of non-milk extrinsic sugars. The range of intakes within each age and sex group was large. For example, for women aged 19 to 24 years, intake at the lower 2.5 percentile was 1g per day while intake at the upper 2.5 percentile was 151g per day.

(Table 3.8)

The current UK recommendation is that the population average intake of non-milk extrinsic sugars should not exceed 10% of total dietary energy or 11% of food energy[2]. As shown in Table 3.9 the mean proportion of food energy from non-milk extrinsic sugars was above the current recommendations for both men and women in this survey, 13.6% and 11.9% respectively, and for all age groups except women aged 50 to 64 years.

Men obtained a significantly higher proportion of food energy from non-milk extrinsic sugars than did women (p<0.01), although comparing men and women within age groups a significant difference is only found for those aged 25 to 34 years (p<0.05). The youngest group of men and women obtained the largest proportion of food energy from non-milk extrinsic sugars, 17.4% and 14.2% respectively, and this was significantly higher than for those aged 50 to 64 years, 12.2% and 11.0% (p<0.05). Indeed, the youngest group of men obtained a significantly higher proportion of their food energy from this source than men in any other age group. At the upper 2.5 percentile of the distribution respondents obtained about 30% of their food energy from non-milk extrinsic sugars, among the youngest group of men this was 36%.

(Table 3.9)

Table 3.10 shows that the main food sources of non-milk extrinsic sugars for both men and women were drinks and sugar, preserves & confectionery, each of which provided about one third of total intake.

The proportion of non-milk extrinsic sugars intake provided by drinks was significantly higher for men than women, 39% compared with 32% (p<0.05). Within this group, carbonated soft drinks, not low calorie, were the main source of non-milk extrinsic sugars, accounting for 12% of intake overall. This was closely followed, for men only, by beer & lager, which contributed 12%. The proportion of non-milk extrinsic sugars provided by drinks decreased with age for both sexes from 57% and 56% for men and women aged 19 to 24 years to 30% and 23% for men and women aged 50 to 64 years (p<0.01). This was largely due to the decrease with age in the contribution of carbonated soft drinks, not low calorie. Indeed, among women drinks accounted for a significantly higher proportion of non-milk extrinsic sugars intake for those aged 19 to 24

years than for all other age groups (25 to 34: p<0.05; 35 to 64: p<0.01).

Within the sugar, preserves & confectionery group, table sugar was the major source of non-milk extrinsic sugars, providing 19% of intake overall. The proportion of non-milk extrinsic sugars intake provided by sugar, preserves & confectionery did not vary significantly with age.

Cereals & cereal products provided 19% of intake of non-milk extrinsic sugars overall. This group accounted for a significantly lower proportion of intake for women aged 19 to 24 years than for those aged 50 to 64 years, 11% and 26% respectively (p<0.05).

(Table 3.10)

Intrinsic and milk sugars

Mean daily intrinsic and milk sugars intake was 39g (median 34g) for men and 37g (median 34g) for women. There were no significant differences between men and women in mean daily intrinsic and milk sugars intake. Mean intake increased with age for both men and women, from 25g and 26g respectively for those aged 19 to 24 years to 46g for men and 44g for women aged 50 to 64 years (p<0.05). Indeed, the youngest group of men had a significantly lower mean daily intake of intrinsic and milk sugars than men in any other age group (p<0.01). Among women, the two youngest groups had a significantly lower mean intake than the two oldest groups of women (p<0.01). In addition, women aged 35 to 49 years had a significantly lower mean daily intake of intrinsic and milk sugars than those aged 50 to 64 years (p<0.05).

As for intakes of non-milk extrinsic sugars there was a large difference within age and sex groups between median and mean values, indicating that there are a small number of cases within each group with relatively large intakes[3]. There was also a wide range of intakes within each age and sex group. For example, for women aged 50 to 64 years, intake at the lower 2.5 percentile was 12g per day compared with 89g per day at the upper 2.5 percentile.

(Table 3.11)

Table 3.12 shows that the major sources of intrinsic and milk sugars were fruit & nuts which accounted for 30% of intake and milk & milk products which accounted for 29% of intake. Reduced fat milks accounted for the largest proportion of intake in the milk & milk products group, 18%. Cereals & cereal products contributed a further 18% to the intake of intrinsic and milk sugars, with bread accounting for about half of this.

The contribution from fruit & nuts increased significantly with age from 14% of intake for men and 23% for women aged 19 to 24 years to 32% and 41% of intake for men and women aged 50 to 64 (p<0.05). This was the only significant difference by age.

(Table 3.12)

3.3.2 Intrinsic sugars, milk sugars and starch

This group includes starch and all sugars with the exception of non-milk extrinsic sugars as previously defined (*see* section 3.3.1 above); that is, total carbohydrates minus non-milk extrinsic sugars.

The COMA Panel on Dietary Reference Values recommended that starches and intrinsic and milk sugars should provide on average 39% of food energy for the population[2]. Table 3.13 shows that on average men obtained 34.9% and women 37.0% of their food energy from this group of carbohydrates (p<0.01). Within age groups, men aged 25 to 34 and 35 to 49 years derived a significantly lower proportion of their food energy from intrinsic and milk sugars and starch than women of the same age (25 to 34: p<0.05; 35 to 49: p<0.01). The youngest group of men derived a significantly lower proportion of their food energy from intrinsic and milk sugars and starch, 32.6%, than those aged 35 to 49 years, 35.1%, and those aged 50 to 64 years, 35.9% (35 to 49: p<0.05; 50 to 64: p<0.01). There were no significant age differences for women.

For all sex and age groups the mean percentage food energy derived from starch and intrinsic and milk sugars fell below the recommendation of 39%. At the upper 2.5 percentile intrinsic and milk sugars and starch provided about half of food energy intake. At the lower 2.5 percentile nearly a quarter of food energy was obtained from this source.

(Table 3.13)

3.3.3 Non-starch polysaccharides (NSP)

The COMA Panel on Dietary Reference Values proposed that the diet of the adult population should contain on average 18g per day non-starch polysaccharides, with an individual range of 12g per day to 24g per day, from a variety of foods[2].

As Table 3.14 shows, the mean daily intake of non-starch polysaccharides was 15.2g for men and significantly lower, 12.6g, for women (p<0.01). In all age groups, apart from those aged 19 to 24 years, men had significantly higher mean intakes of non-starch polysaccharides than women (p<0.01). The youngest group of men had significantly lower mean intakes of non-starch polysaccharides than those in any other age group (25 to 34: p<0.05; all others: p<0.01); in addition, those aged 25 to 34 years had a significantly lower intake than those aged 50 to 64 years (p<0.05). Among women, those aged 19 to 34 years had significantly lower mean intakes of non-starch polysaccharides than those aged 35 to 64 years (25 to 34 compared with 35 to 49: p<0.05; all others: p<0.01). For example, men and women aged 19 to 24 years had mean intakes of 12.3g and 10.6g respectively compared to 16.4g for men and 14.0g for women aged 50 to 64 years (p<0.01). Median values were generally close to the mean within sex and age groups.

All sex and age groups had a mean intake of non-starch polysaccharides below the recommended average intake of 18g per day. A third of men and half the women had intakes below 12g per day.

(Table 3.14)

Table 3.15 shows that the three main sources of non-starch polysaccharides, accounting for about three-quarters of intake, were cereals & cereal products (42%), vegetables (excluding potatoes) (20%) and potatoes & savoury snacks (16%). Within the cereals & cereal products group, whole grain & high fibre breakfast cereals provided 11% of the intake and white bread provided a further 9%.

There were no significant sex or age differences in the proportion of non-starch polysaccharides provided by different food types.

(Table 3.15)

3.4 Variation in intake of protein, total carbohydrate and non-starch polysaccharides

Tables 3.16 and 3.17 show mean and median intakes of protein, total carbohydrate, non-milk extrinsic sugars and non-starch polysaccharides for different groups of respondents in the sample (*see* caveat to section 2.3). Mean and median values are also presented for the percentage of food energy derived from protein, total carbohydrate and non-milk extrinsic sugars.

3.4.1 Region

There were very few regional differences in mean daily intakes, or in the proportion of food energy derived from these nutrients for men or women[4]. The only significant difference was for women living in the Northern region who derived a significantly higher proportion of food energy from total carbohydrate than those living in London and the South East, 49.5% compared with 47.7% (p<0.05). The proportion of food energy derived from non-milk extrinsic sugars exceeded the recommendation of 11% for men and women in each region except for women in London and the South East.

(Table 3.16)

3.4.2 Household receipt of benefits

Men and women living in households receiving state benefits had significantly lower mean daily intakes of protein and non-starch polysaccharides than those in non-benefit households[5]. For example, men and women living in benefit households had a mean daily intake of protein of 79.6g and 56.0g respectively compared with 89.6g and 65.2g for those in non-benefit households (women: p<0.05; men: p<0.01). Mean daily intake of non-starch polysaccharides for men in benefit households was 13.1g and for women 10.5g, compared with 15.5g and 13.0g for those in non-benefit households (p<0.01). There were no significant differences in the mean daily intakes of total carbohydrates or non-milk extrinsic sugars by household benefit status for men or women.

For both sexes, in benefit and non-benefit households, the mean proportion of food energy that came from non-milk extrinsic sugars was higher than the recommendation of 11%. The proportion derived from this source was significantly higher for women in benefit households, 13.6%, than those in non-benefit households, 11.5% (p<0.05). Additionally, women living in benefit households derived a significantly lower proportion of their food energy from protein, 15.8%, than those in non-benefit households, 16.7% (p<0.05). There were no significant differences by household benefit status for men in the proportion of food energy that came from protein or non-milk extrinsic sugars, or for men and women for total carbohydrate.

(Table 3.17)

References and endnotes

[1]   Non-starch polysaccharides refer to non-alpha-glucans as measured by the technique of Englyst and Cummings. Englyst HN, Cummings JH. Improved method for measurement of dietary fibre as non-starch polysaccharides in plant foods. *J Assoc Of Anal Chem* 1988; **71**: 808–814.

[2]   Department of Health. Report on Health and Social Subjects: 41. *Dietary Reference Values for Food Energy and Nutrients for the United Kingdom*. HMSO (London, 1991).

[3]   For each sex and age group the distribution of data was evaluated using the skewness statistic in SPSS. If the skewness statistic was less than twice the standard error of the statistic then data were considered to be normally distributed.

[4]   The areas included in each of the four analysis 'regions' are given in the response chapter, Chapter 2 of the Technical Report, online at http://www.food.gov.uk/ science. Definitions of 'regions' are given in the glossary (*see* Appendix C).

[5]   Households receiving benefits are those where someone in the respondent's household was currently receiving Working Families Tax Credit or had, in the previous 14 days, drawn Income Support or (Income-related) Job Seeker's Allowance. Definitions of 'household' and 'benefits (receiving)', are given in the glossary (*see* Appendix C).

Table 3.1

Average daily protein intake (g) by sex and age of respondent

Cumulative percentages

Average daily protein intake (g)	Age (years):				All
	19–24	25–34	35–49	50–64	
	cum %	cum %	cum %	cum %	cum %
Men					
Less than 45.0	6	0	2	3	2
Less than 53.3	12	2	6	6	6
Less than 55.5	12	5	7	7	7
Less than 65.0	23	19	13	14	16
Less than 75.0	45	33	22	28	30
Less than 85.0	64	49	41	47	48
Less than 95.0	83	70	64	60	67
Less than 105.0	92	83	78	76	80
Less than 115.0	99	91	86	84	89
Less than 125.0	100	94	92	94	94
All		100	100	100	100
Base	*108*	*219*	*253*	*253*	*833*
Mean (average value)	77.8	90.6	90.1	88.8	88.2
Median value	76.1	85.8	88.0	88.6	86.9
Lower 2.5 percentile	34.0	53.8	47.7	41.5	47.1
Upper 2.5 percentile	111.3	156.2	139.9	132.3	135.0
Standard deviation	18.78	50.98	23.27	22.92	32.67
	cum %	cum %	cum %	cum %	cum %
Women					
Less than 35.0	7	7	4	2	4
Less than 45.0	16	20	10	8	13
Less than 46.5	20	21	12	9	14
Less than 55.0	37	43	27	20	30
Less than 65.0	65	69	48	45	54
Less than 75.0	84	86	74	70	77
Less than 85.0	93	95	90	86	90
Less than 95.0	99	98	96	96	97
Less than 105.0	100	99	99	100	99
All		100	100		100
Base	*104*	*210*	*318*	*259*	*891*
Mean (average value)	59.9	58.7	65.1	67.4	63.7
Median value	59.8	59.4	65.5	66.6	63.4
Lower 2.5 percentile	22.8	30.5	29.7	37.3	29.9
Upper 2.5 percentile	90.0	90.2	100.3	99.4	96.0
Standard deviation	16.31	15.73	16.87	15.92	16.61

Table 3.2

Average daily protein intake as a percentage of Reference Nutrient Intake (RNI) by sex and age of respondent

Percentages

Sex and age of respondent	Average daily intake as % of RNI*			Base
	Mean	Median	sd	
Men aged (years):				
19–24	140	137	34	108
25–34	163	155	92	219
35–49	162	159	42	253
50–64	166	166	43	253
All	161	157	59	833
Women aged (years):				
19–24	133	133	36	104
25–34	131	132	35	210
35–49	145	146	37	318
50–64	145	144	35	259
All	140	140	36	891

Note: * The Reference Nutrient Intakes (RNIs) for protein are:

Men: 19 to 50 years: 55.5g/d   Women: 19 to 50 years: 45.0g/d

50+ years: 53.3g/d   50+ years: 46.5g/d

Protein intake as a percentage of RNI was calculated for each respondent using the RNI appropriate for age and sex. The values were then pooled to give the mean, median and sd for each age and sex group.

Table 3.3

Percentage of food energy from protein by sex and age of respondent

Percentage of food energy from protein	Age (years):				All
	19-24	25–34	35–49	50–64	
	cum %	cum %	cum %	cum %	cum %
Men					
10.0 or less	2	2	0	0	1
12.0 or less	14	7	1	3	5
14.0 or less	33	21	17	19	21
16.0 or less	72	53	44	40	49
18.0 or less	88	74	70	67	72
20.0 or less	97	88	90	82	88
22.0 or less	97	96	95	92	94
All	100	100	100	100	100
Base	*108*	*219*	*253*	*253*	*833*
Mean (average value)	14.9	16.5	16.7	17.0	16.5
Median	14.8	15.9	16.3	16.6	16.1
Lower 2.5 percentile	10.2	10.8	12.2	11.9	11.3
Upper 2.5 percentile	22.2	24.2	23.1	25.1	23.4
Standard deviation	2.60	4.73	2.90	3.37	3.63
	cum %	cum %	cum %	cum %	cum %
Women					
10.0 or less	1	1	1	0	1
12.0 or less	16	15	7	3	9
14.0 or less	35	33	22	12	23
16.0 or less	62	57	45	35	47
18.0 or less	83	76	68	58	69
20.0 or less	88	87	84	80	84
22.0 or less	95	95	93	91	93
All	100	100	100	100	100
Base	*104*	*210*	*318*	*259*	*891*
Mean (average value)	15.4	15.9	16.7	17.4	16.6
Median	15.3	15.6	16.4	17.2	16.3
Lower 2.5 percentile	10.3	10.4	11.1	11.6	10.6
Upper 2.5 percentile	23.4	24.4	24.5	24.4	24.2
Standard deviation	3.55	3.60	3.49	3.19	3.50

Table 3.4

Percentage contribution of food types to average daily protein intake by sex and age of respondent

Percentages

Type of food	Men aged (years):				All men	Women aged (years):				All women	All
	19–24	25–34	35–49	50–64		19–24	25–34	35–49	50–64		
	%	%	%	%	%	%	%	%	%	%	%
Cereals & cereal products	24	23	22	23	23	23	25	23	22	23	23
of which:											
pizza	4	2	1	1	2	3	2	1	1	1	2
bread	12	12	13	13	12	12	12	11	10	11	12
breakfast cereals	2	3	3	3	3	2	3	3	4	3	3
Milk & milk products	11	14	15	16	15	15	17	18	18	17	16
of which:											
whole milk	1	2	2	2	2	3	3	2	2	2	2
reduced fat milks	5	6	7	7	6	6	7	8	9	8	7
cheese (incl. cottage cheese)	4	4	4	5	5	4	6	4	5	5	5
yogurt	1	1	1	1	1	1	1	2	2	2	1
Eggs & egg dishes	3	3	3	4	3	3	3	3	3	3	3
Fat spreads	0	0	0	0	0	0	0	0	0	0	0
Meat & meat products	43	39	39	36	38	38	32	33	31	33	36
of which:											
bacon & ham	5	4	5	6	5	3	4	4	4	4	4
beef, veal & dishes	7	7	7	7	7	8	5	7	6	7	7
lamb & dishes	2	2	2	2	2	1	1	2	2	2	2
pork & dishes	2	3	3	4	3	2	2	3	3	2	3
coated chicken & turkey	3	2	2	1	1	3	2	2	1	2	2
chicken, turkey & dishes	12	13	12	10	12	12	12	12	11	11	12
burgers & kebabs	6	3	2	0	2	4	2	1	0	1	2
sausages	3	2	2	2	2	2	2	1	1	1	2
meat pies & pastries	2	2	2	2	2	1	1	2	1	1	2
Fish & fish dishes	3	4	6	8	6	6	6	8	11	8	7
of which:											
white fish (coated, fried and other white fish)	2	2	3	4	3	2	2	3	4	3	3
oily fish	1	2	3	4	3	3	3	4	5	4	3
Vegetables (excluding potatoes)	4	4	5	5	4	5	6	5	5	5	5
Potatoes and savoury snacks	5	4	4	4	4	6	5	4	4	4	4
of which:											
chips	3	2	1	1	2	3	2	1	1	1	2
other potatoes	1	1	2	2	1	2	2	2	2	2	2
Fruit & nuts	0	1	1	2	1	1	1	2	2	2	2
Sugar, preserves & confectionery	1	1	1	1	1	1	1	1	1	1	1
Drinks*	2	3	2	2	2	1	1	1	1	1	2
Miscellaneous**	1	1	1	1	1	1	2	2	2	2	1
Average daily intake (g)	77.8	90.6	90.1	88.8	88.2	59.9	58.7	65.1	67.4	63.7	75.3
Total number of respondents	108	219	253	253	833	104	210	318	259	891	1724

Note: * Includes soft drinks, alcoholic drinks, tea, coffee and water.

** Includes powdered beverages (except tea and coffee), soups, sauces, condiments and artificial sweeteners.

Table 3.5

Average daily total carbohydrate intake (g) by sex and age of respondent

Cumulative percentages

Average daily carbohydrate intake (g)	Age (years):				All
	19–24	25–34	35–49	50–64	
	cum %	cum %	cum %	cum %	cum %
Men					
Less than 150	1	2	5	6	4
Less than 200	13	16	13	19	16
Less than 250	39	38	38	42	39
Less than 300	71	64	65	68	66
Less than 350	90	88	84	86	86
Less than 400	98	96	92	94	95
All	100	100	100	100	100
Base	*108*	*219*	*253*	*253*	*833*
Mean (average value)	273	277	279	269	275
Median	277	275	269	262	269
Lower 2.5 percentile	169	154	130	125	135
Upper 2.5 percentile	390	454	494	452	452
Standard deviation	62	75	86	80	79
	cum %	cum %	cum %	cum %	cum %
Women					
Less than 100	2	3	3	4	3
Less than 150	20	20	18	17	18
Less than 200	44	52	47	48	48
Less than 250	80	85	77	80	80
Less than 300	92	97	94	96	95
All	100	100	100	100	100
Base	*104*	*210*	*318*	*259*	*891*
Mean (average value)	206	196	206	203	203
Median	209	199	208	204	203
Lower 2.5 percentile	104	97	87	78	90
Upper 2.5 percentile	322	304	334	317	317
Standard deviation	61	53	61	61	59

Table 3.6

Percentage of food energy from total carbohydrate by sex and age of respondent

Cumulative percentages

Percentage of food energy from carbohydrate	Age (years):				All
	19–24	25–34	35–49	50–64	
	cum %	cum %	cum %	cum %	cum %
Men					
35.0 or less	-	2	1	1	1
40.0 or less	7	9	10	12	10
45.0 or less	32	31	34	35	33
50.0 or less	51	66	68	64	64
55.0 or less	86	88	90	91	89
60.0 or less	97	100	98	98	98
All	100		100	100	100
Base	*108*	*219*	*253*	*253*	*833*
Mean (average value)	49.0	47.7	47.5	47.4	47.7
Median	49.7	48.2	47.6	47.3	48.0
Lower 2.5 percentile	38.0	35.2	36.0	35.6	35.9
Upper 2.5 percentile	63.2	58.3	59.9	59.5	59.8
Standard deviation	6.29	5.84	5.88	6.17	6.03
	cum %	cum %	cum %	cum %	cum %
Women					
35.0 or less	1	2	2	4	2
40.0 or less	6	7	9	11	9
45.0 or less	22	23	28	29	26
50.0 or less	52	60	58	58	58
55.0 or less	81	88	85	86	85
60.0 or less	95	96	96	98	96
All	100	100	100	100	100
Base	*104*	*210*	*318*	*259*	*891*
Mean (average value)	49.1	48.7	48.6	48.1	48.5
Median	49.0	48.2	48.4	48.8	48.4
Lower 2.5 percentile	36.5	36.6	35.3	32.2	34.7
Upper 2.5 percentile	62.7	61.9	62.4	59.4	61.5
Standard deviation	8.25	5.78	6.78	6.67	6.72

Table 3.7

Percentage contribution of food types to average daily total carbohydrate intake by sex and age of respondent

Percentages

Type of food	Men aged (years):				All men	Women aged (years):				All women	All
	19–24	25–34	35–49	50–64		19–24	25–34	35–49	50–64		
	%	%	%	%	%	%	%	%	%	%	%
Cereals & cereal products	39	46	45	48	45	39	45	45	45	44	45
of which:											
rice	3	4	4	3	3	3	4	4	3	3	3
bread	19	22	22	23	22	19	21	20	19	20	21
breakfast cereals	4	7	7	8	7	6	7	8	9	8	7
biscuits	2	3	3	4	3	2	3	4	4	3	3
buns, cakes & pastries	3	3	4	5	4	2	4	4	5	4	4
Milk & milk products	4	5	6	6	5	6	6	7	8	7	6
of which:											
whole milk	0	1	1	1	1	1	1	1	1	1	1
reduced fat milks	2	2	3	3	3	2	3	3	4	3	3
Eggs & egg dishes	0	0	0	0	0	0	0	0	0	0	0
Fat spreads	0	0	0	0	0	0	0	0	0	0	0
Meat & meat products	6	6	5	5	5	6	5	5	4	4	5
Fish & fish dishes	1	1	1	1	1	1	1	1	1	1	1
Vegetables (excluding potatoes)	4	3	4	4	4	3	5	5	4	4	4
Potatoes and savoury snacks	14	12	11	11	12	16	13	12	11	12	12
of which:											
chips	7	5	4	4	5	7	5	4	3	4	4
other fried or roast potatoes	1	1	1	1	1	1	1	1	1	1	1
other potatoes	3	4	4	5	4	5	5	6	6	6	5
savoury snacks	3	2	2	1	2	3	3	2	1	2	2
Fruit & nuts	1	3	5	6	4	3	5	7	10	7	5
Sugar, preserves & confectionery	9	9	10	9	10	8	8	9	8	9	9
of which:											
table sugar	4	6	6	6	6	3	4	5	4	4	5
chocolate confectionery	3	3	2	1	2	3	3	3	2	3	2
Drinks*	20	13	10	8	11	16	9	7	6	8	10
of which:											
fruit juice	1	1	2	2	2	2	2	2	2	2	2
carbonated soft drinks,											
not low calorie	11	5	2	1	4	9	3	2	1	3	3
other soft drinks	2	1	1	1	1	2	2	1	1	1	1
beer and lager	3	4	3	3	4	1	1	1	0	1	2
Miscellaneous**	2	2	2	2	2	1	2	3	3	2	2
Average daily intake (g)	273	277	279	269	275	206	196	206	203	203	273
Total number of respondents	108	219	253	253	833	104	210	318	259	891	1724

Note: * Includes soft drinks, alcoholic drinks, tea, coffee and water.

** Includes powdered beverages (except tea and coffee), soups, sauces, condiments and artificial sweeteners.

Table 3.8

Average daily non–milk extrinsic sugars intake (g) by sex and age of respondent

Cumulative percentages

Average daily non–milk extrinsic sugars intake (g)	Age (years):				All
	19–24	25–34	35–49	50–64	
	cum %	cum %	cum %	cum %	cum %
Men					
Less than 20	–	3	6	7	4
Less than 40	5	15	15	23	16
Less than 60	27	36	41	44	39
Less than 80	36	56	60	68	58
Less than 100	56	74	77	80	74
Less than 120	67	84	87	89	84
Less than 140	83	90	92	93	91
Less than 160	93	94	95	97	95
All	100	100	100	100	100
Base	*108*	*219*	*253*	*253*	*833*
Mean (average value)	96	80	78	70	79
Median	95	75	71	65	71
Lower 2.5 percentile	32	15	12	12	14
Upper 2.5 percentile	210	192	198	163	188
Standard deviation	43.1	43.2	47.1	39.2	43.9
	cum %	cum %	cum %	cum %	cum %
Women					
Less than 10	7	5	4	6	5
Less than 20	12	16	12	15	14
Less than 40	31	44	44	44	42
Less than 60	58	68	68	74	68
Less than 80	75	86	85	88	85
Less than 100	86	94	92	96	93
Less than 120	92	97	96	98	96
All	100	100	100	100	100
Base	*104*	*210*	*318*	*259*	*891*
Mean (average value)	60	49	51	48	51
Median	54	44	43	44	44
Lower 2.5 percentile	1	6	6	5	5
Upper 2.5 percentile	151	125	134	112	129
Standard deviation	38.4	29.8	33.5	30.9	32.7

Table 3.9

Percentage of food energy from non-milk extrinsic sugars by sex and age of respondent

Cumulative percentages

Percentage of food energy from non-milk extrinsic sugars	Age (years):				All
	19–24	25–34	35–49	50–64	
	cum %	cum %	cum %	cum %	cum %
Men					
10.0 or less	20	32	36	39	34
11.0 or less*	25	38	44	46	40
15.0 or less	41	62	68	71	64
20.0 or less	62	84	86	90	84
25.0 or less	89	92	94	97	94
30.0 or less	96	96	98	100	98
All	100	100	100		100
Base	*108*	*219*	*253*	*253*	*833*
Mean (average value)	17.4	13.9	13.1	12.2	13.6
Median	17.2	12.7	12.0	11.8	12.5
Lower 2.5 percentile	5.9	3.1	3.4	2.7	3.3
Upper 2.5 percentile	35.7	30.8	29.3	26.9	29.3
Standard deviation	7.35	6.76	6.52	5.85	6.68
	cum %	cum %	cum %	cum %	cum %
Women					
10.0 or less	32	41	46	45	43
11.0 or less*	36	49	54	54	51
15.0 or less	61	74	77	81	75
20.0 or less	74	92	91	94	90
25.0 or less	87	96	96	99	96
30.0 or less	98	97	98	99	98
All	100	100	100	100	100
Base	*104*	*210*	*318*	*259*	*891*
Mean (average value)	14.2	11.8	11.8	11.0	11.9
Median	12.6	11.3	10.7	10.4	10.9
Lower 2.5 percentile	0.2	2.0	2.4	2.0	1.9
Upper 2.5 percentile	29.4	30.8	29.9	23.4	28.3
Standard deviation	7.63	6.26	6.79	5.76	6.54

*Note: * The current recommendation is that intake of non-milk extrinsic sugars should not exceed 11% of food energy .*

Table 3.10

Percentage contribution of food types to average daily non–milk extrinsic sugars intake by sex and age of respondent

Percentages

Type of food	Men aged (years):				All men	Women aged (years):				All women	All
	19–24	25–34	35–49	50–64		19–24	25–34	35–49	50–64		
	%	%	%	%	%	%	%	%	%	%	%
Cereals & cereal products	10	16	18	22	18	11	20	23	26	21	19
of which:											
high fibre & whole grain breakfast cereals	1	3	3	3	2	2	2	3	5	3	3
other breakfast cereals	2	2	2	2	2	2	3	3	2	2	2
biscuits	2	5	5	5	4	3	4	6	5	5	5
buns, cakes & pastries	4	5	6	8	6	2	7	7	9	7	6
Milk & milk products	3	4	4	4	4	5	5	5	7	6	5
Eggs & egg dishes	0	0	0	0	0	0	0	0	1	0	0
Fat spreads	0	0	0	0	0	0	0	0	0	0	0
Meat & meat products	1	1	1	1	1	1	1	1	1	1	1
Fish & fish dishes	0	0	0	0	0	0	0	0	0	0	0
Vegetables (excluding potatoes)	2	1	1	1	1	1	2	1	1	1	1
Potatoes and savoury snacks	0	0	0	0	0	0	0	0	0	0	0
Fruit & nuts	0	1	1	2	1	0	1	1	3	2	1
Sugar, preserves & confectionery	24	30	35	34	32	24	32	35	33	32	32
of which:											
table sugar	12	20	23	22	20	10	16	18	17	16	19
preserves & sweet spreads	1	1	3	6	3	1	4	4	5	4	3
sugar confectionery	3	1	2	1	2	3	2	3	4	3	2
chocolate confectionery	8	7	7	5	7	8	9	9	7	8	7
Drinks*	57	44	35	30	39	56	35	29	23	32	37
of which:											
fruit juice	3	4	6	7	5	7	8	7	9	8	7
carbonated soft drinks not low calorie	31	17	8	4	13	29	12	8	5	11	12
concentrated soft drinks not low calorie	3	2	2	2	2	5	3	2	1	2	2
ready to drink still soft drinks not low calorie	3	1	1	1	1	3	3	3	2	3	2
beer and lager	10	15	12	12	12	5	4	3	1	3	9
alcopops	3	0	0	0	1	4	1	1	0	1	1
Miscellaneous**	3	3	3	4	3	2	5	5	5	5	4
Average daily intake (g)	96	80	78	70	79	60	49	51	48	51	64
Total number of respondents	108	219	253	253	833	104	210	318	259	891	1724

Note: * Includes soft drinks, alcoholic drinks, tea, coffee and water.

** Includes powdered beverages (except tea and coffee), soups, sauces, condiments and artificial sweeteners.

Table 3.11

Average daily intrinsic and milk sugars intake (g) by sex and age of respondent

Cumulative percentages

Average daily intrinsic and milk sugars intake (g)	Age (years):				All
	19–24	25–34	35–49	50–64	
	cum %	cum %	cum %	cum %	cum %
Men					
Less than 10	1	1	1	2	1
Less than 15	17	6	4	4	6
Less than 30	76	48	34	24	40
Less than 45	90	76	63	56	68
Less than 60	96	91	84	74	84
Less than 75	100	96	94	90	94
All		100	100	100	100
Base	*108*	*219*	*253*	*253*	*833*
Mean (average value)	25	36	42	46	39
Median	22	30	38	42	34
Lower 2.5 percentile	10	13	12	11	11
Upper 2.5 percentile	61	80	95	89	89
Standard deviation	13.4	20.6	21.2	22.2	21.5
	cum %	cum %	cum %	cum %	cum %
Women					
Less than 10	4	2	1	1	1
Less than 15	24	10	8	5	10
Less than 30	68	53	39	23	41
Less than 45	90	85	67	60	72
Less than 60	98	95	87	77	87
Less than 75	100	100	97	94	97
All			100	100	100
Base	*104*	*210*	*318*	*259*	*891*
Mean (average value)	26	31	38	44	37
Median	24	30	37	40	34
Lower 2.5 percentile	7	12	11	12	11
Upper 2.5 percentile	55	62	78	89	77
Standard deviation	12.9	13.8	18.1	20.3	18.4

Table 3.12

Percentage contribution of food types to average daily intrinsic and milk sugars intake by sex and age of respondent

Percentages

Type of food	Men aged (years):				All men	Women aged (years):				All women	All
	19–24	25–34	35–49	50–64		19–24	25–34	35–49	50–64		
	%	%	%	%	%	%	%	%	%	%	%
Cereals & cereal products	24	21	18	19	20	18	17	15	14	15	18
of which:											
bread	*13*	*10*	*9*	*8*	*10*	*9*	*8*	*7*	*6*	*7*	*8*
breakfast cereals	*2*	*4*	*3*	*4*	*3*	*3*	*3*	*3*	*4*	*3*	*3*
buns, cakes & pastries	*2*	*1*	*2*	*4*	*3*	*1*	*2*	*2*	*2*	*2*	*2*
Milk & milk products	29	32	30	27	30	32	29	30	27	29	29
of which:											
whole milk	*3*	*8*	*6*	*5*	*6*	*8*	*7*	*5*	*3*	*5*	*6*
reduced fat milks	*20*	*19*	*18*	*16*	*18*	*17*	*16*	*18*	*18*	*17*	*18*
yogurt	*3*	*3*	*3*	*3*	*3*	*3*	*4*	*4*	*4*	*4*	*3*
Eggs & egg dishes	0	0	0	0	0	0	0	0	0	0	0
Fat spreads	0	0	0	0	0	0	0	0	0	0	0
Meat & meat products	9	6	5	4	5	6	5	4	2	4	4
Fish & fish dishes	1	0	0	0	0	0	0	0	0	0	0
Vegetables (excluding potatoes)	10	10	10	11	10	10	12	11	10	11	10
Potatoes and savoury snacks	5	3	3	3	3	5	3	2	2	3	3
Fruit & nuts	14	22	29	32	27	23	29	32	41	33	30
Sugar, preserves & confectionery	4	3	2	1	2	3	2	2	1	2	2
Drinks*	0	1	1	0	1	0	0	1	1	0	1
Miscellaneous**	2	2	1	2	2	1	2	2	1	2	2
Average daily intake (g)	**25**	**36**	**42**	**46**	**39**	**26**	**31**	**38**	**44**	**37**	**38**
Total number of respondents	**108**	**219**	**253**	**253**	**833**	**104**	**210**	**318**	**259**	**891**	**1724**

Note: * *Includes soft drinks, alcoholic drinks, tea, coffee and water.*
  ** *Includes powdered beverages (except tea and coffee), soups, sauces, condiments and artificial sweeteners.*

Table 3.13

Percentage of food energy from intrinsic and milk sugars and starch by sex and age of respondent

Cumulative percentages

Percentage of food energy from intrinsic and milk sugars and starch	Age (years):				All
	19–24	25–34	35–49	50–64	
	cum %	cum %	cum %	cum %	cum %
Men					
25.0 or less	7	5	5	3	5
30.0 or less	36	26	20	15	22
35.0 or less	70	50	50	44	51
39.0 or less	88	74	75	72	76
40.0 or less	88	83	81	79	82
45.0 or less	100	95	93	92	94
50.0 or less		99	99	98	99
All		100	100	100	100
Base	*108*	*219*	*253*	*253*	*833*
Mean (average value)	32.6	34.7	35.1	35.9	34.9
Median	31.2	34.8	35.0	35.9	34.9
Lower 2.5 percentile	23.5	24.1	22.4	24.8	23.7
Upper 2.5 percentile	44.4	46.4	47.3	48.0	47.4
Standard deviation	5.49	6.25	6.30	5.87	6.13
	cum %	cum %	cum %	cum %	cum %
Women					
25.0 or less	5	4	3	5	4
30.0 or less	21	13	13	13	14
35.0 or less	39	35	37	35	36
39.0 or less	72	60	63	61	63
40.0 or less	78	65	67	65	68
45.0 or less	93	88	87	87	88
50.0 or less	98	97	97	98	97
All	100	100	100	100	100
Base	*104*	*210*	*318*	*259*	*891*
Mean (average value)	35.5	37.3	37.1	37.3	37.0
Median	36.3	36.9	36.6	36.7	36.6
Lower 2.5 percentile	21.0	22.9	23.5	22.5	22.5
Upper 2.5 percentile	46.5	51.3	51.6	50.0	50.8
Standard deviation	7.26	6.78	6.80	6.82	6.87

Table 3.14

Average daily non–starch polysaccharides intake (g) by sex and age of respondent

Average daily non–starch polysaccharides intake (g)	Age (years):				All
	19–24	25–34	35–49	50–64	
	cum %	cum %	cum %	cum %	cum %
Men					
Less than 6.0	6	0	2	1	2
Less than 8.0	16	8	8	6	8
Less than 10.0	33	23	19	14	20
Less than 12.0	42	38	30	25	32
Less than 14.0	68	50	44	38	47
Less than 16.0	89	66	60	49	62
Less than 18.0	94	77	70	61	72
Less than 20.0	96	87	79	72	81
Less than 22.0	97	90	84	84	87
Less than 24.0	100	94	89	89	92
All		100	100	100	100
Base	*108*	*219*	*253*	*253*	*833*
Mean (average value)	12.3	14.6	15.7	16.4	15.2
Median	12.7	14.0	15.0	16.1	14.3
Lower 2.5 percentile	5.1	6.8	6.0	6.5	6.2
Upper 2.5 percentile	22.7	28.7	31.4	29.1	28.9
Standard deviation	3.93	6.00	6.48	5.93	6.04
	cum %	cum %	cum %	cum %	cum %
Women					
Less than 6.0	9	6	7	5	6
Less than 8.0	25	23	16	10	17
Less than 10.0	52	39	29	22	32
Less than 12.0	67	57	47	41	50
Less than 14.0	79	76	65	57	67
Less than 16.0	92	86	77	70	79
Less than 18.0	96	92	85	80	87
Less than 20.0	99	96	92	88	92
Less than 22.0	100	97	95	92	95
All		100	100	100	100
Base	*104*	*210*	*318*	*259*	*891*
Mean (average value)	10.6	11.6	12.8	14.0	12.6
Median	9.7	11.1	12.3	13.0	12.0
Lower 2.5 percentile	3.9	4.9	4.7	5.4	5.0
Upper 2.5 percentile	18.5	23.7	24.0	28.8	24.2
Standard deviation	3.72	4.52	4.98	5.44	5.01

Table 3.15

Percentage contribution of food types to average daily non–starch polysaccharides intake by sex and age of respondent

Percentages

Type of food	Men aged (years):				All men	Women aged (years):				All women	All
	19–24	25–34	35–49	50–64		19–24	25–34	35–49	50–64		
	%	%	%	%	%	%	%	%	%	%	%
Cereals & cereal products	39	45	44	43	43	38	40	41	41	40	42
of which:											
pasta	3	3	2	1	2	4	3	2	1	2	2
pizza	5	3	1	1	2	2	2	1	1	1	1
white bread	13	11	11	10	11	11	9	8	7	8	9
wholemeal bread	3	6	6	6	6	2	5	6	6	5	6
other bread	4	5	4	5	5	5	5	4	4	4	5
high fibre & whole grain breakfast cereals	5	11	11	11	11	7	8	12	16	12	11
other breakfast cereals	2	1	1	1	1	2	2	1	1	1	1
Milk & milk products	0	0	0	0	0	0	0	1	1	0	0
Eggs & egg dishes	0	0	0	0	0	0	0	0	0	0	0
Fat spreads	0	0	0	0	0	0	0	0	0	0	0
Meat & meat products	10	8	7	6	7	7	6	6	4	5	6
Fish & fish dishes	1	1	1	1	1	1	1	1	1	1	1
Vegetables (excluding potatoes)	19	18	20	21	20	18	22	22	21	21	20
of which:											
baked beans	10	5	5	3	5	4	4	3	2	3	4
Potatoes and savoury snacks	23	17	15	14	16	24	17	15	13	15	16
of which:											
chips	11	6	5	4	6	9	6	4	3	5	5
other fried or roast potatoes	2	1	1	1	1	2	1	1	1	1	1
other potatoes	6	6	6	7	6	8	7	7	7	7	7
savoury snacks	5	3	3	1	3	5	4	2	1	2	2
Fruit & nuts	3	7	10	11	9	8	9	12	16	12	10
Sugar, preserves & confectionery	1	1	1	1	1	2	1	1	1	1	1
Drinks*	0	0	0	0	0	0	0	0	0	0	0
Miscellaneous**	2	2	2	3	2	2	2	2	2	2	2
Average daily intake (g)	12.3	14.6	15.7	16.4	15.2	10.6	11.6	12.8	14.0	12.6	13.8
Total number of respondents	108	219	253	253	833	104	210	318	259	891	1724

Note: * Includes soft drinks, alcoholic drinks, tea, coffee and water.

    ** Includes powdered beverages (except tea and coffee), soups, sauces, condiments and artificial sweeteners.

Table 3.16

Average daily intake of protein, carbohydrates and non-starch polysaccharides (g) and percentage food energy from protein and carbohydrates by sex of respondent and region

Grams and percentages

Nutrient	Region											
	Scotland			Northern			Central, South West and Wales			London and the South East		
	Mean	Median	sd	Mean	Median	sd	Mean	Median	sd	Mean	Median	sd
Men												
Protein (g)	93.3	91.0	22.76	86.7	87.1	24.73	89.7	86.8	45.09	86.6	84.5	21.83
Protein as % food energy	17.5	16.6	3.12	16.8	16.7	3.32	16.1	15.7	4.25	16.4	16.1	3.11
Total carbohydrate (g)	271	264	80	266	263	70	285	279	87	271	269	74
Total carbohydrate as % food energy	46.5	46.4	5.12	48.1	48.5	6.20	47.8	48.2	5.59	47.6	47.6	6.56
Non-milk extrinsic sugars (g)	67	53	49.6	77	69	42.2	85	75	46.4	75	72	39.8
Non-milk extrinsic sugars as % food energy	11.6	10.5	6.43	13.8	12.5	7.07	14.3	13.3	6.59	13.2	12.2	6.36
Non-starch polysaccharides (g)	15.7	14.4	6.74	14.3	13.6	5.44	15.5	14.4	6.26	15.6	14.8	6.06
Base		65			234			294			240	
Women												
Protein (g)	62.8	59.6	15.40	63.1	62.9	18.42	63.9	63.3	14.87	64.1	64.6	17.34
Protein as % food energy	16.8	16.9	3.05	16.7	16.6	3.40	16.6	16.1	3.53	16.5	16.0	3.67
Total carbohydrate (g)	198	185	54	202	199	58	206	207	60	201	207	60
Total carbohydrate as % food energy	48.6	47.4	5.60	49.5	49.3	5.78	48.6	48.4	6.89	47.7	48.3	7.38
Non-milk extrinsic sugars (g)	50	45	28.2	51	46	31.3	54	45	37.9	47	44	27.3
Non-milk extrinsic sugars as % food energy	12.4	12.0	6.06	12.1	10.9	6.74	12.3	11.2	7.19	11.0	10.2	5.53
Non-starch polysaccharides (g)	12.0	11.7	4.34	12.4	11.8	5.23	12.5	12.1	4.82	13.0	12.4	5.17
Base		66			229			327			268	

Table 3.17

Average daily intake of protein, carbohydrates and non-starch polysaccharides (g) and percentage food energy from protein and carbohydrates by sex of respondent and whether someone in respondent's household was receiving certain benefits

Grams and percentages

Nutrient	Whether receiving benefits					
	Receiving benefits			Not receiving benefits		
	Mean	Median	sd	Mean	Median	sd
Men						
Protein (g)	79.6	76.0	25.99	89.6	87.5	33.38
Protein as % food energy	15.8	15.5	3.46	16.6	16.1	3.64
Total carbohydrate (g)	259	262	74	277	269	79
Total carbohydrate as % food energy	48.4	48.8	6.61	47.6	47.9	5.93
Non-milk extrinsic sugars (g)	76	70	42.9	79	72	44.1
Non-milk extrinsic sugars as % food energy	14.5	13.9	8.04	13.5	12.5	6.45
Non-starch polysaccharides (g)	13.1	12.5	5.55	15.5	14.7	6.05
Base		110			723	
Women						
Protein (g)	56.0	54.0	18.48	65.2	64.9	15.77
Protein as % food energy	15.8	15.7	3.50	16.7	16.4	3.48
Total carbohydrate (g)	193	193	70	205	206	57
Total carbohydrate as % food energy	49.7	49.7	6.83	48.3	48.3	6.67
Non-milk extrinsic sugars (g)	56	48	41.9	50	44	30.5
Non-milk extrinsic sugars as % food energy	13.6	12.3	8.64	11.5	10.7	5.98
Non-starch polysaccharides (g)	10.5	9.6	4.82	13.0	12.5	4.94
Base		150			741	

4 Alcohol intake

4.1 Introduction

For adults, sustained excessive consumption of alcohol has the effect of increasing the risk of high blood pressure and stroke. It is also a recognised risk factor for other conditions, for example cancers and cirrhosis of the liver[1]. Current advice for adults is that men should drink no more than three to four units of alcohol a day and women no more than two to three units a day[2,3]. Consistently drinking four or more units a day for men, or three or more units a day for women, is not advised as a sensible drinking level because of the progressive health risk it carries. This advice applies particularly to young adults (aged 16 to 24 years), as 'binge drinking' is a common and hazardous pattern of drinking in this age group.

Information on alcohol consumption was collected as part of the dietary interview and also recorded in the seven-day dietary diary. The percentage of total energy derived from alcohol is also presented, and differences in alcohol intake by region and household benefit status are examined. As a considerable number of respondents said they did not drink alcohol, or did not record any alcohol in the dietary record, data are presented both including non-consumers (that is for the total sample) and excluding them (for consumers only).

It should be noted that the data collected in the dietary interview relate to the consumption of alcoholic drinks only, while data from the dietary record may also include alcohol consumed as part of recipe dishes. Data collected in the dietary interview are used to calculate weekly consumption of alcohol in units. As the revised guidelines focus on maximum daily consumption of alcohol we cannot simply divide weekly consumption by seven as this would give average daily consumption. It was decided, therefore, to use the information recorded in the dietary record to estimate maximum daily units consumed.

4.2 Data from the dietary interview

As part of the dietary interview respondents were asked if they drank alcohol at all. Those who said they did were then asked how often over the last 12 months they had drunk different types of alcohol (beer, shandy, wine, fortified wines, spirits and alco-pops) and how much they had usually drunk on any one day. This information is combined to give an estimate of the respondent's weekly alcohol consumption[4].

Table 4.1 shows that 5% of men and 10% of women reported never having an alcoholic drink (p<0.01). The proportion who said they did not drink increased significantly with age for women but not for men. For example, 5% of the youngest group of women said they did not drink alcohol compared with 14% of those aged 50 to 64 years (p<0.05).

Among those who said that they had consumed an alcoholic drink during the last 12 months (that is, consumers only), men reported drinking an average of 22.3 units of alcohol a week compared with 10.0 units for women (p<0.01). The mean number of units consumed weekly decreased with age among both men and women. The youngest group of men consumers drank a significantly higher mean number of units of alcohol a week, 28.3 units, than those aged 50 to 64 years, 19.6 units (p<0.01). Among women consumers, those aged 19 to 24 years had a significantly higher mean weekly consumption of alcohol than any other age group, and reported drinking nearly twice as many units as those aged 35 to 64 years (25 to 34 years: p<0.05; 35 to 64 years: p<0.01). Additionally, women aged 25 to 34 years reported drinking a significantly higher mean number of units of alcohol than those aged 50 to 64 years (p<0.01).

Table 4.2 shows weekly alcohol consumption for the NDNS sample compared with data from the 2000 General Household Survey (GHS)[5]. In the GHS sample, a significantly higher proportion of men, but not women, reported not drinking alcohol, 8% of men in the GHS compared with 5% in the NDNS (p<0.05). These differences between the NDNS and GHS may result from the fact that in the GHS interviews are carried out with all adults in the household and the NDNS with only one randomly selected adult. It is therefore more likely that the GHS interview takes place in the presence of other household members, and for this reason GHS respondents may be more reticent in talking about their alcohol consumption.

(Tables 4.1 and 4.2)

4.3   Data from the dietary record

Data on alcohol intake from the dietary record are presented as average daily intake in grams in Table 4.3 and as percentage of total energy in Table 4.4. Maximum daily intake in units is shown in Table 4.6 and discussed in section 4.4. Weekly intake in units is shown in Tables 4.7(a) and 4.7(b) and compared with data from the dietary interview in section 4.5.

Overall, 81% of men and 69% of women had consumed drinks or other items containing alcohol during the seven-day dietary recording period (p<0.01). There were no significant differences by age for either men or women.

Men had a significantly higher mean daily intake of alcohol than women. This was true within each age group and for both the total sample and consumers only. Mean daily intake of alcohol was 21.9g for men (27.2g for consumers only) and 9.3g for women (13.5g for consumers only) (p<0.01). There were no significant age differences in mean daily intake of alcohol for men or women.

As would be expected, the distribution of alcohol intake was positively skewed and median values were considerably lower than mean values.

As shown in Table 4.4, the percentage of total energy derived from alcohol shows a similar pattern to that for absolute intakes. Men obtained a significantly greater percentage of total energy from alcohol than women. This was true within each age group and for both the total sample and

consumers only. Overall, men obtained 6.5% of their total energy from alcohol (8.1% for consumers only) and women, 3.9% (5.7% for consumers only) (p<0.01). There were no significant age differences in the percentage of total energy derived from alcohol for men or women.

Median values were considerably lower than mean values, for the total sample and consumers only, indicating that the data are positively skewed with a small number of respondents deriving a large percentage of their total energy from alcohol. At the upper 2.5 percentile, women consumers derived close to one fifth of total energy from alcohol and men consumers one quarter. There was little variation with age.

(Tables 4.3 and 4.4)

4.4   Maximum daily consumption of alcohol

This section discusses maximum daily consumption of alcohol during the seven-day recording period. Data from the dietary record includes alcohol intake from food and from alcoholic drinks. Alcohol from food contributed an average of 1.5% to total alcohol intake, and to ensure consistency with the GHS data, was excluded from this analysis. The day with the highest recorded consumption of alcohol from drinks was used to derive maximum daily consumption[6].

The following focuses on:

● the proportions exceeding the recommended daily benchmarks, that is more than four units a day for men and more than three for women; and

● those who consumed more than eight units a day for men and six for women, defined as heavy drinking[7].

These measures are the same as those used in the GHS, and 2000 GHS data are provided for comparative purposes.

Table 4.5 shows the number of days on which consumption of alcohol exceeded the daily benchmarks. Overall, 60% of men and 44% of women consumed more than the recommended benchmark on at least one day during the dietary recording period (p<0.01). Three per cent of men and less than 0.5% of women consumed more than the daily benchmarks on every day of the dietary recording period (p<0.01).

Table 4.6 shows the maximum daily amount of alcohol consumed by sex and age. Men were significantly more likely than women to have exceeded the daily benchmarks on at least one day during the dietary recording period (p<0.01). Men aged 35 to 49 years and women aged 19 to 24 years were significantly more likely to have exceeded the daily benchmarks than those aged 50 to 64 years (p<0.05).

Thirty-nine per cent of men consumed more than eight units and 22% of women more than six units of alcohol on their heaviest drinking day (p<0.01). There were no significant age differences in the proportion of men consuming more than eight units on any one day. Among women those aged 19 to 34 years were significantly more likely than the oldest group of women to have consumed more than six units on their heaviest drinking day (19 to 24 years: p<0.05; 25 to 34 years: p<0.01).

Compared with data from the 2000 GHS, men and women in the NDNS were significantly more likely to have consumed more than the daily benchmarks and to have consumed more than eight/six units on their heaviest drinking day. For example, 44% of women in the NDNS consumed more than three units of alcohol on at least one day, including 22% who had consumed more than six units, compared with 28% and 11% respectively of women in the GHS (p<0.01).

These differences were also seen in most age/sex groups. For example, men and women aged 25 to 64 years in the NDNS were significantly more likely than those in the GHS to have consumed more than the daily benchmarks on their heaviest drinking day (men and women aged 25 to 34 years: p<0.05: all others: p<0.01). Men aged 35 to 64 years, and women aged 25 to 64 years, in the NDNS were significantly more likely than those in the GHS to have consumed more than eight/six units on their heaviest drinking day (p<0.01).

The differences between the NDNS and the GHS may be due to differences in the method of recording alcohol consumption and in calculating maximum daily amount. The GHS asks respondents as part of the face-to-face interview how much of each of six types of drink they had drunk on their heaviest drinking day during the previous week. These amounts are then added to give an estimate of the most the respondent had drunk on any one day. In the NDNS maximum daily amount was derived from information the respondent recorded in the dietary diary. In addition, as shown in Table 4.2, the proportion of men and women drinking more than 21/14 units a

week, derived from the dietary interview data, was significantly higher in the NDNS than in the GHS (p<0.05). This suggests that in both the dietary interview and the dietary record the NDNS recorded higher levels of consumption than the GHS.

(Tables 4.5 and 4.6)

4.5 Comparing data from the dietary interview with data from the dietary record

There are a number of similarities in alcohol consumption patterns between the dietary interview data and the information from the dietary record, and a number of differences. In both data sources, men were more likely than women to be drinkers and to have consumed a significantly higher mean number of units than women. However, age differences in alcohol consumption evident in the interview data were not seen in the dietary record data. This may reflect the different methods of collecting the information and the different reference periods, the past 12 months in the interview, previous seven days in the dietary record. It may also be indicative of possible response bias in the dietary record sample, if those who drank larger amounts of alcohol were unwilling to complete a dietary record or under-reported their consumption. Equally, the interview data may be over-reported; for example the youngest group may have exaggerated consumption.

Tables 4.7(a) and 4.7(b) compare the mean number of units consumed weekly calculated from the interview data with the number of units recorded in the seven-day dietary diary for the total sample and consumers only. Interview data are presented only for those who kept a dietary record.

Interview data classify a respondent as a non-drinker if they say that they do not drink at all, whereas the dietary record classifies respondents as non-drinkers if there is no record of alcohol consumption during the seven-day recording period. Occasional drinkers could therefore be classified as drinkers from the interview data, but as non-drinkers from their dietary record. The proportion of men and women classified as non-drinkers from the dietary record, 19% and 31%, is significantly higher than from the interview, 5% and 10% (p<0.01).

Overall, the mean weekly number of units of alcohol consumed calculated from interview data did not differ significantly from that recorded in the dietary record. This was true for men and women, total sample and consumers only.

For consumers only, mean weekly consumption for the two oldest groups of women was significantly lower in the interview data, 8.6 and 7.7 units respectively, than in the dietary record data, 11.6 and 11.2 (p<0.05). This suggests that these women either under-reported their consumption of alcohol at the interview or over-reported their consumption in the dietary record. There were no significant differences for men. In addition, age differences in alcohol consumption seen for men from the interview data did not exist when these data were examined for those who completed the dietary record only. One possible explanation might be that young men who drank larger amounts of alcohol were unwilling to complete a dietary record.

(Tables 4.7(a) and 4.7(b))

4.6   Variation in intake of alcohol

Tables 4.8 and 4.9 show mean alcohol intakes, from the dietary record data, for different groups of respondents in the sample (*see* caveat to section 2.3). Data are presented for the total sample and consumers only.

4.6.1   Region

Generally there were few significant regional differences in the proportion of men and women who recorded consuming alcohol during the seven-day dietary recording period[8]. Men in the Northern region were more likely than those living in London and the South East to have consumed alcohol, 83% and 71% respectively (p<0.05).

There were no significant regional differences for men or women in mean daily alcohol intake or in the proportion of total energy derived from alcohol.

(Table 4.8)

4.6.2   Household receipt of benefits

Men and women living in households in receipt of benefits were significantly less likely than those in non-benefit households to have recorded consuming alcohol during the dietary recording period[9]. For example, 59% of men and 55% of women in benefit households recorded consuming alcohol compared with 84% of men and 71% of women in non-benefit households (p<0.01).

Among consumers only there was no significant difference in mean daily intake of alcohol by household benefit status for men or women.

The percentage of total energy derived from alcohol shows a similar pattern to that for absolute intakes. Among consumers only, there was no significant difference in the percentage of total energy derived from alcohol by household benefit status for men or women.

(Table 4.9)

References and endnotes

[1]   Alcohol Concern. *Factsheet 8: Health impacts of alcohol.* **35**. Winter 2002/03.

[2]   Department of Health. *Sensible drinking - the report of an inter-departmental working group.* HMSO (London, 1996).

[3]   One unit of alcohol is approximately equivalent to half a pint of beer, lager or cider, a single measure of spirits, one glass of wine or one small glass of sherry, port or other fortified wine. One unit is equivalent to 8g of alcohol consumed.

[4]   Quantities were converted to units according to the type of alcoholic drink, and weekly consumption of alcohol in units was calculated using the definition and method used by the General Household Survey 2000.

[5]   The General Household Survey (GHS) is a multi-purpose continuous survey carried out by the Social Survey Division of the Office for National Statistics (ONS) which collects information on a range of topics from people living in private households in Great Britain. The 2000 GHS was carried out between April 2000 and March 2001: the set sample size was 13,250 and the response rate was 67%. Comparison data is for all 19 to 64 year old respondents to the 2000 GHS: 11,400 unweighted and 34,733,471 weighted and grossed. Walker A, Maher J, Coulthard M, Goddard E, Thomas M. *Living in Britain: Results from the 2000 General Household Survey.* TSO (London, 2001).

[6]   One unit is equal to 8g of alcohol. Units of alcohol are calculated by dividing the amount of alcohol recorded in the dietary diary in grams by 8.

[7]   These measures are those used in the GHS to discuss the proportions exceeding the daily benchmarks and the proportion who have drunk heavily, defined as eight units for men and six for women. GHS respondents were asked about their alcohol consumption in the week prior to interview.

[8]   The areas included in each of the four analysis 'regions' are given in the response chapter, Chapter 2 of the Technical Report, online at http://www.food.gov.uk/science. Definitions of 'regions' are given in the glossary (*see* Appendix C).

[9]   Households receiving benefits are those where someone in the respondent's household was currently receiving Working Families Tax Credit or had, in the previous 14 days, drawn Income Support or (Income-related) Job Seeker's Allowance. Definitions of 'household' and 'benefits (receiving)' are given in the glossary (*see* Appendix C).

Table 4.1

Weekly alcohol consumption (units) as reported in the dietary interview by sex and age of respondent

Responding sample   Percentages

Reported weekly alcohol consumption (units)*	Total sample aged (years):				All	Consumers aged (years):				All
	19–24	25–34	35–49	50–64		19–24	25–34	35–49	50–64	
	%	%	%	%	%	%	%	%	%	%
(a) Men										
Non-drinker	2	4	6	7	5	-	-	-	-	-
Less than 1 unit	5	2	4	6	4	5	2	4	6	4
1–10 units	25	34	29	37	32	26	35	30	40	34
11–21 units	15	19	29	22	22	15	20	31	24	24
22–35 units	27	21	16	11	17	28	22	18	12	18
36–50 units	12 ⎱53	10 ⎱41**	10 ⎱33	9 ⎱29**	10 ⎱36	12 ⎱54	10 ⎱43	10 ⎱35	10 ⎱31	10 ⎱38
51 or more units	14	11	7	8	9	14	11	7	9	10
Mean number of units	27.8	21.6	20.7	18.3	21.1	28.3	22.5	22.0	19.6	22.3
Base	*142*	*287*	*330*	*330*	*1088*	*139*	*274*	*311*	*308*	*1032*
	%	%	%	%	%	%	%	%	%	%
(b) Women										
Non-drinker	5	8	10	14	10	-	-	-	-	-
Less than 1 unit	7	9	13	17	12	7	10	14	20	14
1–7 units	21	35	39	38	36	22	38	43	45	40
8–14 units	20	23	21	16	20	21	25	24	18	22
15–25 units	30	16	11	9	14	32	18	13	11	16
26–35 units	6 ⎱47	5 ⎱25	3 ⎱17	4 ⎱15**	4 ⎱22	7 ⎱50	5 ⎱27	3 ⎱19	5 ⎱17	5 ⎱24**
36 or more units	11	4	3	1	4	11	4	3	1	4
Mean number of units	16.2	10.0	8.0	6.5	9.0	17.1	10.9	8.9	7.6	10.0
Base	*136*	*275*	*415*	*337*	*1163*	*129*	*253*	*371*	*289*	*1042*

Note: * Weekly guidelines were set at a maximum number of 21 units of alcohol a week for men, and 14 units a week for women. Current guidelines are a maximum daily amount of 4 units for men and 3 units for women.

    ** In order to avoid rounding errors, the combined percentage has been calculated separately and may differ by one percentage point from the sum of the percentages in the individual categories.

Table 4.2

Weekly alcohol consumption (units) as reported in the dietary interview compared with data from the 2000 General Household Survey

Percentages

Reported weekly alcohol consumption (units)*	NDNS responding sample		2000 General Household Survey**	
	Total sample	Consumers only	All aged 19–64	Consumers only
	%	%	%	%
(a) Men				
Non–drinker	5	-	8	-
Less than 1 unit	4	4	6	6
1–10 units	32	34	32	35
11–21units	22	24	23	25
22–35 units	17	18	15	17
36–50 units	10 36	10 38	8 30	9 34
51 or more units	9	10	7	8
Base	*1088*	*1032*	*4986*	*4626*
	%	%	%	%
(b) Women				
Non–drinker	10	-	11	-
Less than 1 unit	12	14	14	16
1–7 units	36	40	39	43
8–14 units	20	22	18	20
15–25 units	14	16	12	14
26–35 units	4 22	5 24***	3 18	4 22
36 or more units	4	4	3	4
Base	*1163*	*1042*	*5628*	*5046*

Note: *   Weekly guidelines were set at a maximum number of 21 units of alcohol a week for men, and 14 units a week for women.
Current guidelines are a maximum daily amount of 4 units for men and 3 units for women.

** 2000 General Household Survey: weighted data from adults aged 19 to 64 years.

*** In order to avoid rounding errors, the combined percentage has been calculated separately and may differ by one percentage point from the sum of the percentages in the individual categories.

Table 4.3

Average daily alcohol intake (g) by sex and age of respondent

Diary sample   Cumulative percentages

Average daily alcohol intake (g)	Men aged (years):				All men	Women aged (years):				All women
	19–24	25–34	35–49	50–64		19–24	25–34	35–49	50–64	
	cum %	cum %	cum %	cum %	cum %	cum %	cum %	cum %	cum %	cum %
(a) Total sample										
Zero	20	18	16	23	19	29	31	31	33	31
Less than 1.0	22	19	17	25	21	29	33	34	38	34
Less than 2.0	25	23	18	29	24	37	39	39	43	40
Less than 5.0	30	31	29	36	32	48	49	49	58	51
Less than 10.0	46	40	39	44	42	64	65	67	67	66
Less than 15.0	60	48	45	58	52	71	77	78	76	76
Less than 20.0	64	62	54	65	61	78	87	85	83	84
Less than 30.0	75	73	70	74	73	88	94	94	94	93
Less than 40.0	80	80	81	79	80	93	99	97	97	97
Less than 50.0	87	85	86	87	86	97	99	99	100	99
Less than 60.0	95	89	91	90	91	99	99	99		100
All	100	100	100	100	100	100	100	100		
Base	*108*	*219*	*253*	*253*	*833*	*104*	*210*	*318*	*259*	*891*
Mean (average value)	20.4	22.2	23.1	21.1	21.9	11.4	9.1	9.2	8.6	9.3
Median	10.6	16.0	18.4	13.0	14.1	6.0	5.5	5.3	3.5	4.7
Upper 2.5 percentile	78.7	81.2	82.2	95.8	83.5	55.1	37.7	41.7	41.0	41.0
Standard deviation	25.35	24.18	23.88	25.81	24.72	14.48	11.26	12.14	11.45	12.05
(b) Consumers only										
Percentage consumers	80%	82%	84%	77%	81%	71%	69%	69%	67%	69%
Mean (average value)	25.6	27.2	27.4	27.5	27.2	16.1	13.2	13.2	12.9	13.5
Median	15.8	18.4	21.4	18.6	19.7	10.1	10.4	9.5	9.1	9.8
Upper 2.5 percentile	78.7	83.4	88.6	97.9	88.0	57.6	38.2	46.6	43.1	44.9
Standard deviation	25.94	24.09	23.63	26.30	24.80	14.87	11.41	12.61	11.87	12.44
Base	*86*	*179*	*213*	*194*	*673*	*74*	*145*	*220*	*174*	*613*

Table 4.4

Percentage of total energy from alcohol by sex and age of respondent

Diary sample   Cumulative percentages

Percentage of total energy from alcohol	Men aged (years):				All men	Women aged (years):				All women
	19–24	25–34	35–49	50–64		19–24	25–34	35–49	50–64	
	cum %	cum %	cum %	cum %	cum %	cum %	cum %	cum %	cum %	cum %
(a) Total sample										
Zero	20	18	16	23	19	29	31	31	33	31
1 or less	27	25	21	33	27	35	42	39	45	41
2 or less	36	33	32	38	35	48	48	47	56	50
5 or less	59	50	46	57	52	63	66	71	73	70
10 or less	79	78	74	75	76	84	88	89	88	88
15 or less	91	86	88	88	87	94	98	96	97	97
All	100	100	100	100	100	100	100	100	100	100
Base	108	219	253	253	833	104	210	318	259	891
Mean (average value)	6.0	6.6	6.8	6.4	6.5	4.6	4.0	3.9	3.7	3.9
Median	3.6	5.1	5.6	4.0	4.4	2.1	2.2	2.2	1.5	2.0
Upper 2.5 percentile	26.2	25.6	23.6	28.4	25.6	18.9	14.9	16.7	16.1	16.8
Standard deviation	7.50	7.01	6.92	7.53	7.20	5.54	4.81	5.30	4.92	5.11
(b) Consumers only										
Mean (average value)	7.6	8.1	8.1	8.3	8.1	6.4	5.8	5.6	5.4	5.7
Median	5.5	6.1	6.4	5.8	6.1	5.1	4.7	4.1	4.1	4.3
Upper 2.5 percentile	27.3	25.8	24.1	29.9	25.8	20.8	16.2	18.8	19.6	18.9
Standard deviation	7.68	6.95	6.83	7.60	7.19	5.60	4.81	5.56	5.13	5.27
Base	86	179	213	194	673	74	145	220	174	613

Table 4.5

Number of days on which units of alcohol consumed exceeded the daily benchmarks by sex and age of respondent*

Diary sample   Percentages

Number of days on which units of alcohol consumed exceeded recommended daily benchmarks*	Men aged (years):				All men	Women aged (years):				All women
	19–24	25–34	35–49	50–64		19–24	25–34	35–49	50–64	
	%	%	%	%	%	%	%	%	%	%
0	35	38	35	48	40	43	53	56	64	56
1	33	18	18	11	18	26	22	20	10	18
2	12	18	15	11	14	16	11	10	11	11
3	12	7	13	9	10	7	8	7	5	7
4	6	7	7	4	6	5	4	3	5	4
5	–	8	5	7	6	2	1	2	3	2
6	1	4	3	4	3	–	0	1	1	1
7	1	0	4	5	3	–	–	0	1	0
Base	108	219	253	253	833	104	210	318	259	891

Note: * Recommended daily benchmarks are no more than 4 units of alcohol for men and 3 units of alcohol for women.

Table 4.6

Maximum daily amount of alcohol consumed from alcoholic beverages (units) during seven-day dietary recording period by sex and age of respondent

Diary sample   Percentages

Maximum daily amount	Age of respondent (years):									
	2000/01 NDNS				All	GHS 2000*				All
	19–24	25–34	35–49	50–64		19–24	25–34	35–49	50–64	
	%	%	%	%	%	%	%	%	%	%
Men										
Drank nothing during last seven days**	20	19	17	24	20	24	22	22	23	23
Up to 4 units	14	19	18	24	20	23	29	36	40	34
More than 4, up to 8 units	15 ⎫65	22 ⎫62	25 ⎫65	19 ⎫52	21 ⎫60	13 ⎫53	18 ⎫49	19 ⎫42	21 ⎫37***	19 ⎫43
More than 8 units	50 ⎭	40 ⎭	40 ⎭	33 ⎭	39 ⎭	40 ⎭	31 ⎭	23 ⎭	15 ⎭	24 ⎭
Mean number of units	9.4	8.3	8.2	6.3	7.8	..	..	..	..	..
Base	108	219	253	253	833	491	1052	1835	1610	4988
	%	%	%	%	%	%	%	%	%	%
Women										
Drank nothing during last seven days**	29	32	33	35	33	32	33	33	40	35
Up to 3 units	14	21	23	29	23	23	33	40	42	37
More than 3, up to 6 units	23 ⎫57	17 ⎫47***	23 ⎫44	22 ⎫36	21 ⎫44***	16 ⎫44	19 ⎫34	17 ⎫27***	13 ⎫17	16 ⎫28***
More than 6 units	34 ⎭	29 ⎭	21 ⎭	14 ⎭	22 ⎭	28 ⎭	15 ⎭	9 ⎭	4 ⎭	11 ⎭
Mean number of units	5.3	4.0	3.6	2.7	3.6	..	..	..	..	..
Base	104	210	318	259	891	544	1307	2061	1724	5636

Note: *   2000 General Household Survey: weighted data from adults aged 19 to 64 years.

** For the NDNS, alcohol consumption is calculated from items recorded in the seven-day dietary diary. GHS respondents were asked about alcohol consumption in the week prior to interview.

*** In order to avoid rounding errors, the combined percentage has been calculated separately and may differ by one percentage point from the sum of the percentages in the individual categories.

Table 4.7(a)

Weekly alcohol consumption (units) as reported in the dietary interview and the seven–day dietary record by sex and age of respondent: total diary sample (including non–consumers)

Diary sample (including non–consumers)

Percentages

Average weekly alcohol consumption (units)*	Interview data: respondents aged (years):**				All	Dietary record data: respondents aged (years):				All
	19–24	25–34	35–49	50–64		19–24	25–34	35–49	50–64	
	%	%	%	%	%	%	%	%	%	%
Men										
Non–drinker	1	4	6	6	5	20	18	16	23	19
Less than 1 unit	6	1	3	6	4	–	1	1	2	1
1–10 units	26	38	30	38	34	31	25	25	24	26
11–21 units	20	18	30	21	23	19	26	21	20	22
22–35 units	22	20	16	12	17	10	10	18	9	12
36–50 units	17	10	8	8	10	14	9	9	11	10
51 or more units	8	9	7	8	8	5	11	10	10	10
	46***	39	32***	28	35	30***	30	37	31***	32
Mean number of units	25.5	20.6	21.0	17.8	20.5	17.9	19.4	20.2	19.5	19.2
Base	108	219	253	253	833	108	219	253	253	833
Women										
Non–drinker	5	9	10	12	10	29	31	31	33	31
Less than 1 unit	7	8	15	18	13	–	1	2	3	2
1–7 units	22	33	39	39	36	29	28	29	29	29
8–14 units	20	25	21	15	20	15	19	18	12	16
15–25 units	24	17	10	9	13	14	14	12	16	14
26–35 units	8	5	3	5	5	7	6	4	4	5
36 or more units	14	3	3	1	4	7	1	3	3	3
	46	25	16	15	21***	27***	21	20***	23	22
Mean number of units	17.6	10.0	7.8	6.8	9.1	10.0	7.9	8.0	7.6	8.1
Base	104	210	318	259	891	104	210	318	259	891

Note: * Weekly guidelines were set at a maximum number of 21 units of alcohol a week for men, and 14 units a week for women. Current guidelines are a maximum daily amount of 4 units for men and 3 units for women.

** Weekly alcohol consumption as recorded in the dietary interview is presented for those who completed the dietary record only .

*** In order to avoid rounding errors, the combined percentage has been calculated separately and may differ by one percentage point from the sum of the percentages in the individual categories.

Table 4.7(b)

Weekly alcohol consumption (units) as reported in the dietary interview and the seven-day dietary record by sex and age of respondent: diary sample consumers only

Diary sample (consumers only) Percentages

Average weekly alcohol consumption (units)*	Interview data: consumers aged (years):**				All	Dietary record data: consumers aged (years):				All
	19–24	25–4	35–49	50–64		19–24	25–34	35–49	50–64	
	%	%	%	%	%	%	%	%	%	%
Men										
Less than 1 unit	7	1	3	7	4	–	1	1	2	1
1–10 units	26	39	32	41	36	39	30	30	32	32
11–21 units	20	19	32	22	24	24	32	25	26	27
22–35 units	22	21	17	13	18	13	12	21	12	15
36–50 units	17 | 47	11 | 41	9 | 34***	9 | 30	10 | 36	18 | 37	11 | 37	10 | 44***	14 | 40	13 | 40
51 or more units	8	9	7	8	8	6	14	12	14	12
Mean number of units	25.9	21.4	22.2	19.0	21.5	22.4	23.8	24.0	24.1	23.8
Base	*107*	*211*	*238*	*238*	*794*	*86*	*179*	*213*	*194*	*672*
Women										
Less than 1 unit	7	9	16	20	14	–	1	3	5	3
1–7 units	23	36	43	45	39	40	40	42	44	42
8–14 units	21	28	24	18	23	21	28	27	18	24
15–25 units	25	18	11	11	14	19	21	18	24	21
26–35 units	9 | 49	5 | 27	3 | 17	6 | 18	5 | 24***	10 | 38***	9 | 30***	6 | 28	5 | 34***	7 | 32
36 or more units	15	4	3	1	4	10	1	4	4	4
Mean number of units	18.6	10.9	8.6	7.7	10.1	14.1	11.5	11.6	11.2	11.8
Base	*99*	*192*	*287*	*227*	*805*	*74*	*145*	*220*	*174*	*613*

Note: * Weekly guidelines were set at a maximum number of 21 units of alcohol a week for men, and 14 units a week for women. Current guidelines are a maximum daily amount of 4 units for men and 3 units for women.

    ** Weekly alcohol consumption as recorded in the dietary interview is presented for those who completed the dietary record only.

    *** In order to avoid rounding errors, the combined percentage has been calculated separately and may differ by one percentage point from the sum of the percentages in the individual categories.

Table 4.8

Average daily intake of alcohol (g) and percentage total energy from alcohol by region and sex of respondent

Diary sample
Grams and percentages

Alcohol	Region											
	Scotland			Northern			Central, South West and Wales			London and the South East		
	Mean	Median	sd	Mean	Median	sd	Mean	Median	sd	Mean	Median	sd
(a) Total sample – Men												
Alcohol (g)	22.0	19.2	20.75	24.4	18.0	27.13	19.9	12.4	22.29	22.0	13.1	25.98
Alcohol as % total energy	6.8	5.6	6.45	7.3	5.6	7.68	5.8	3.8	6.72	6.5	4.1	7.43
Percentage consumers		80%			83%			81%			71%	
Base		65			234			294			240	
(b) Consumers only – Men												
Alcohol (g)	27.5	22.2	19.64	29.3	22.1	27.21	24.6	17.9	22.33	28.1	17.4	26.28
Alcohol as % total energy	8.5	7.3	6.11	8.7	6.9	7.63	7.2	5.5	6.78	8.3	5.6	7.44
Base = all consumers		52			195			237			189	
(a) Total sample – Women												
Alcohol (g)	10.6	8.4	13.27	10.3	4.8	13.86	8.5	4.5	10.90	8.9	3.8	11.38
Alcohol as % total energy	4.8	3.5	6.00	4.3	2.0	5.75	3.6	1.8	4.51	3.8	1.9	4.94
Percentage consumers		70%			67%			69%			70%	
Base		66			229			327			268	
(b) Consumers only – Women												
Alcohol (g)	15.2	10.4	13.53	15.5	11.4	14.44	12.3	9.5	11.18	12.8	9.1	11.66
Alcohol as % total energy	6.9	5.8	6.12	6.5	4.9	5.98	5.2	4.2	4.60	5.4	4.1	5.12
Base = all consumers		46			153			227			187	

Table 4.9

Average daily intake of alcohol (g) and percentage of total energy from alcohol by sex of respondent and whether someone in respondent's household was receiving certain benefits

Diary sample
Grams and percentages

Alcohol	Whether receiving benefits					
	Receiving benefits			Not receiving benefits		
	Mean	Median	sd	Mean	Median	sd
(a) Total sample – Men						
Alcohol (g)	11.7	1.6	23.33	23.5	16.1	24.58
Alcohol as % total energy	3.5	0.7	6.66	7.0	5.1	7.18
Percentage consumers		59%			84%	
Base		110			723	
(b) Consumers only – Men						
Alcohol (g)	19.9	13.2	27.64	27.9	20.0	24.38
Alcohol as % total energy	6.0	3.7	7.78	8.3	6.4	7.09
Base = all consumers		65			608	
(a) Total sample – Women						
Alcohol (g)	8.3	1.6	14.08	9.4	4.9	11.60
Alcohol as % total energy	3.8	0.7	6.56	3.9	2.1	4.76
Percentage consumers		55%			71%	
Base		150			741	
(b) Consumers only – Women						
Alcohol (g)	14.9	11.7	16.10	13.2	9.7	11.76
Alcohol as % total energy	6.9	5.0	7.52	5.5	4.3	4.80
Base = all consumers		83			529	

5 Fat and fatty acids intake

5.1 Introduction

This chapter presents data on the intakes of fat and fatty acids. Data are shown separately for intakes of total fat, saturated, *trans* unsaturated, *cis* monounsaturated and *cis* polyunsaturated fatty acids (n-3 and n-6), and for cholesterol[1].

5.1.1 Current recommendations on fat intakes for adults

Dietary Reference Values (DRVs) for fat and fatty acids have been formulated for adults and are expressed as population averages[2]. Current recommendations are that total fat intake should contribute a population average of no more than 35% of daily food energy intake, that is excluding alcohol (33% of daily total energy intake, including alcohol). Saturated fatty acids should contribute an average of no more than 11% of food energy, *cis* polyunsaturated fatty acids an average of 6.5%, *cis* monounsaturated fatty acids 13%, and *trans* fatty acids an average of no more than 2% of food energy intake for the population. Subsequently, in the Report on Nutritional Aspects of Cardiovascular Disease, the Committee on Medical Aspects of Food Policy (COMA) recommended that in respect of *cis* n-6 polyunsaturated fatty acids there should be no further increase in average intakes and that the proportion of the population with intakes providing more than 10% of their energy should not increase. In respect of average daily intakes of long chain *cis* n-3 polyunsaturated fatty acids COMA recommended an increase from about 0.1g to 0.2g per day[3].

5.2 Total fat

Tables 5.1 and 5.2 show the average daily intake of total fat for men and women and the contribution made by total fat to their food energy intake. The mean daily total fat intake for men was 86.5g and for women, significantly lower, 61.4g (p<0.01). There were no significant differences in the mean daily intakes by age for men or women.

Men derived a mean of 35.8% and women 34.9% of their food energy intake from total fat (p<0.05). There were no significant age differences in the mean percentage of food energy derived from fat for men or women.

As noted in section 5.1.1 the DRV for the population average percentage contribution to food energy intake from total fat for adults is 35%. In this survey, the mean percentage of food energy derived from total fat was above the DRV for men in all age groups, and for women in the two youngest age groups.

(Tables 5.1 and 5.2)

5.3 Saturated fatty acids

Tables 5.3 and 5.4 show the average daily intake of saturated fatty acids for respondents and the contribution made by saturated fatty acids to their food energy intake. Overall men in the survey had a mean daily intake of saturated fatty acids of 32.5g; the mean intake for women was 23.3g (p<0.01). There were no significant differences in mean daily intakes by age for men or women. Intakes at the upper 2.5 percentile were about twice median intakes for all sex and age groups, except for women aged 19 to 24 years where intake at the upper 2.5 percentile was more than three times the median value, 64.6g and 21.1g respectively.

Men derived 13.4% and women 13.2% of their food energy intake from saturated fatty acids (ns). There were no significant age differences for men or women.

For adults, the DRV for the population average percentage contribution to food energy intake from saturated fatty acids is 11%. In this survey the mean proportion of food energy derived from saturated fatty acids was above 11% for each age/ sex group.

(Tables 5.3 and 5.4)

5.4 *Trans* unsaturated fatty acids (*trans* fatty acids)

Tables 5.5 and 5.6 show the average daily intake of *trans* fatty acids for respondents and the contribution made by *trans* fatty acids to their food energy intake. Mean daily intake of *trans* fatty acids for men was 2.91g and for women 2.04g (p<0.01). There were no significant differences in mean daily intakes for men or women by age.

Both men and women derived 1.2% of their food energy from *trans* fatty acids (ns). There were no significant differences by age for men or women.

The DRV set for adults for the population average percentage contribution to food energy intake from *trans* fatty acids is no more than 2%. In this survey, the mean percentage of food energy from *trans* fatty acids for men and women in all age groups was below the reference value.

(Tables 5.5 and 5.6)

5.5 *Cis* monounsaturated fatty acids

Tables 5.7 and 5.8 show the average daily intake of *cis* monounsaturated fatty acids for respondents and the contribution made by *cis* monounsaturated fatty acids to their food energy intake. Mean daily intake of *cis* monounsaturated fatty acids for men was 29.1g and for women 20.2g (p<0.01). Men had significantly higher mean intakes than women in each age group (p<0.01). There were no significant differences by age in the mean daily intake of *cis* monounsaturated fatty acids for men or women.

Men derived 12.1% and women 11.5% of their food energy intake from *cis* monounsaturated fatty acids (p<0.01). There were no significant differences for men or women by age.

The DRV for adults for *cis* monounsaturated fatty acids is that they should provide 13% of food

energy as a population average. Table 5.8 shows that the mean values for men and women in all age groups were below this level.

(Tables 5.7 and 5.8)

5.6 *Cis* polyunsaturated fatty acids

Cis polyunsaturated fatty acids can be divided into two main groups, *cis* n-3 and *cis* n-6 polyunsaturated fatty acids; each group has different biological functions and is found in different foods. Fish oils are the richest source of *cis* n-3 polyunsaturated fatty acids, but they are also found in seed oils and margarine. *Cis* n-6 polyunsaturated fatty acids are mainly found in plant oils including soya, corn and sunflower oils and margarine derived from these oils.

5.6.1 *Cis* n-3 polyunsaturated fatty acids

Table 5.9 shows the average daily intake of *cis* n-3 polyunsaturated fatty acids for respondents. Overall, men had a significantly higher mean daily intake of *cis* n-3 polyunsaturated fatty acids than women, 2.27g (median 2.09g) compared with 1.71g (median 1.55g) (p<0.01). Women aged 25 to 34 years had a significantly lower mean intake of *cis* n-3 polyunsaturated fatty acids than those aged 50 to 64 years, 1.60g and 1.82g respectively (p<0.05). There were no other significant differences in mean daily intake by age for men or women.

Generally, within each age and sex group, there was a large difference between median and mean values[4]. This indicates that there were a small number of cases within each group with relatively large intakes of *cis* n-3 polyunsaturated fatty acids.

(Table 5.9)

5.6.2 *Cis* n-6 polyunsaturated fatty acids

Table 5.10 shows the average daily intake of *cis* n-6 polyunsaturated fatty acids for respondents. The mean daily intake of *cis* n-6 polyunsaturated fatty acids for men was 12.9g (median 12.3g) and for women 9.4g (median 8.9g) (p<0.01). There were no significant differences in mean daily intake by age for men or women.

Generally, within each age and sex group, there was a large difference between median and mean values[4]. This indicates that there were a small number of cases within each group with relatively large intakes of *cis* n-6 polyunsaturated fatty acids.

(Table 5.10)

5.6.3 Percentage energy from *cis* polyunsaturated fatty acids

COMA recommended that the population average intake of *cis* polyunsaturated fatty acids should be 6.5% of food energy intake. Moreover individual intakes should not contribute more than 10% of total energy. For infants, children and adults COMA recommended that linoleic acid (*cis* n-6) should provide at least 1% of total energy and α- linolenic acid (*cis* n-3) at least 0.2% of total energy[2]. As mentioned in Section 5.1.1, COMA recommended that in respect of *cis* n-6 polyunsaturated fatty acids there should be no further increase in average intakes and that the proportion of the population with intakes providing more than 10% of their energy should not increase. In respect of average daily intakes of long chain *cis* n-3 polyunsaturated fatty acids COMA recommended an increase from about 0.1g to 0.2g per day[3].

Table 5.11 shows that in this survey men and women derived 1.0% of their food energy from *cis* n-3 polyunsaturated fatty acids (ns). There were no significant differences by age for men or women.

Table 5.12 shows that men derived a mean of 5.4% and women 5.3% of their food energy intake from *cis* n-6 polyunsaturated fatty acids (ns). Women in the two youngest age groups derived a significantly higher proportion of their food energy from *cis* n-6 polyunsaturated fatty acids, 5.6% for both groups, than the oldest group of women, 5.0% (19 to 24: p<0.05; 25 to 34: p<0.01). There were no significant differences by age for men.

The DRV for α-linolenic acid, part of the *cis* n-3 group, is at least 0.2% of total energy for individuals, and for linoleic acid, part of the *cis* n-6 group, at least 1% of total energy for individuals. The survey did not collect information on intakes of individual fatty acids. However, intakes of *cis* n-3 and *cis* n-6 polyunsaturated fatty acids as a percentage of food energy, at the lower 2.5 percentile of the distribution, were well above the DRVs set for individual fatty acids. This indicates that the percentage of respondents who failed to meet the DRVs is likely to be low.

(Tables 5.11 and 5.12)

5.7 Cholesterol

Dietary cholesterol has a relatively small and variable effect on serum and plasma cholesterol levels and for that reason COMA set no DRV for cholesterol. However, in its Report on Nutritional Aspects of Cardiovascular Disease COMA recommended that average daily population intakes should not rise above the 1992 level of 245mg[3]. The Food and Agriculture Organisation/World Health Organization (FAO/WHO) expert committee on Fats and Oils in Human Nutrition advised 'reasonable restriction' on dietary cholesterol at below 300mg a day; whether this applies to individuals or is a population average is not made clear[5].

Table 5.13 shows the average daily intake of cholesterol for respondents. The mean daily intake of cholesterol for men was 304mg and for women, significantly lower, 213mg (p<0.01). Women aged 19 to 24 years had a significantly lower mean cholesterol intake than those aged 35 to 64 years, in addition those aged 25 to 34 years had a significantly lower intake than the oldest group of women (19 to 24 compared with 50 to 64: p<0.05; all others: p<0.01).

COMA recommended that average daily population intakes of cholesterol should not rise above 245mg. In this survey, mean intake of cholesterol for men, but not women, exceeded this recommendation. This was true across all age groups. The FAO/WHO advised 'reasonable restriction' on dietary cholesterol at below 300mg a day. Mean intake of cholesterol exceeded 300mg for men aged 35 to 64 years. At the upper 2.5 percentile, intakes of cholesterol were above 300mg across all sex and age groups. Indeed, at the upper 2.5 percentile intake for men in each age group was over 600mg per day.

(Table 5.13)

5.8 Sources of fat in diet

5.8.1 Total fat, saturated, *trans* unsaturated and *cis* monounsaturated fatty acids

Tables 5.14 to 5.17 show the percentage contribution of food types to average daily intake of total fat (Table 5.14), saturated (Table 5.15), *trans* unsaturated (Table 5.16) and *cis* monounsaturated fatty acids (Table 5.17) for respondents by sex and age.

The main sources of total fat, saturated, *trans* and *cis* monounsaturated fatty acids in the diets of respondents were cereals & cereal products, milk & milk products, meat & meat products, fat spreads and potatoes & savoury snacks. Men obtained a significantly higher proportion of their intake of saturated fatty acids from meat & meat products than women, 25% compared with 19% (p<0.05). There were no other significant differences in the contribution of major food types to total fat, saturated, *trans* and *cis* monounsaturated fatty acid intakes by sex or age.

Overall, cereals & cereal products accounted for almost a fifth, 19%, of the intake of total fat, a similar proportion, 18%, of saturated fatty acids intake, and 17% of *cis* monounsaturated fatty acids intake. The contribution made by this food type to the intake of *trans* fatty acids was higher at 26%. Within this food group the main sources of fat, saturated, *trans* and *cis* monounsaturated fatty acids were biscuits and buns, cakes & pastries.

Milk & milk products accounted for 14% of total fat intake, 24% of the intake of saturated fatty acids, 16% of *trans* fatty acids and 10% of *cis* monounsaturated fatty acids intake. The main contributor within this food group was cheese.

Fat spreads contributed 12% to the intake of total fat and 11% to the intake of both saturated and *cis* monounsaturated fatty acids. The contribution made by this food type to the intake of *trans* fatty acids was slightly higher, 18% overall. Within the fat spreads group, the principal source of total fat was reduced fat spreads, contributing 5% overall, and for saturated fatty acids was butter, contributing 6%. Non-polyunsaturated reduced fat spreads contributed 7% to intakes of *trans* fatty acids and 4% to total intake of *cis* monounsaturated fatty acids.

Meat & meat products contributed 23% to the intake of total fat, 22% to the intake of saturated fatty acids, 21% to the intake of *trans* fatty acids and 27% to the intake of *cis* monounsaturated fatty acids. Within this food group, beef, veal & dishes, meat pies & pastries and chicken & turkey dishes were the main contributors to intakes of total fat and saturated, *trans* and *cis* monounsaturated fatty acids.

The consumption of potatoes & savoury snacks accounted for 10% of total fat intake, slightly less to the intake of saturated fatty acids, 7%, and *trans* fatty acids, 6%, and slightly more to intake of *cis* monounsaturated fatty acids, 12%.

(Tables 5.14 to 5.17)

5.8.2   *Cis* n-3 and n-6 polyunsaturated fatty acids

Table 5.18 shows the percentage contribution of food types to intakes of *cis* n-3 polyunsaturated fatty acids. The main sources were cereals & cereal products, meat & meat products and potatoes & savoury snacks which each contributed 17% to the intake of *cis* n-3 polyunsaturated fatty acids. Fish & fish dishes contributed a further 14% and vegetables (excluding potatoes) 11%.

There were no significant differences between men and women in the percentage contribution of these food types to intakes of *cis* n-3 polyunsaturated fatty acids.

In the meat & meat products group, chicken & turkey dishes was the main contributor (5%). In the fish & fish products food group, oily fish contributed 10% overall. Potato chips provided the majority of the contribution from potatoes & savoury snacks, providing 12% of total intake overall but over one fifth of the total intake of *cis* n-3 polyunsaturated fatty acids for men and women aged 19 to 24 years, 22% and 20% respectively.

Overall, there were few significant differences in the contribution of these food types to intakes of *cis* n-3 polyunsaturated fatty acids by age. For both men and women, the contribution from fish & fish dishes increased with age from 4% and 6% respectively for those aged 19 to 24 years to 18% and 23% for men and women aged 50 to 64 years (p<0.01). This increase is mainly due to the contribution made by oily fish which was significantly lower in men and women aged 19 to 24 years than in those aged 50 to 64 years (50 to 64 years: p<0.01).

Table 5.19 shows the main sources of *cis* n-6 polyunsaturated fatty acids in the diets of respondents. These were cereals & cereal products, 20%, meat & meat products, 18%, fat spreads, 14%, and potatoes & savoury snacks, 13%. There were no significant differences between men and women or between age groups in the contribution of the major food groups to intakes of *cis* n-6 polyunsaturated fatty acids.

The main source of *cis* n-6 polyunsaturated fatty acids within cereals & cereal products was white bread contributing 4% overall, and within the fat spreads group was polyunsaturated reduced fat spreads, contributing 6% overall. In the meat & meat products food group the main contributor was chicken & turkey dishes providing 5% of intake overall, and in the potatoes & savoury snacks groups, chips which provided 7% of intake.

(Tables 5.18 and 5.19)

5.9   Variation in intake of fat

Tables 5.20 and 5.21 show mean and median intakes of total fat and saturated, *trans*, *cis* monounsaturated, *cis* n-3 polyunsaturated and *cis* n-6 polyunsaturated fatty acids for different groups of respondents in the sample (see caveat to Section 2.3). Mean and median values are also presented for the percentage of food energy derived from total fat and these fatty acids.

5.9.1 Region

There were few significant regional differences for men or women in mean daily intakes of total fat or fatty acids[6]. Men in the Northern region had significantly lower mean daily intakes of total fat and saturated, *trans* and *cis* monounsaturated fatty acids than men in Central and South West regions of England and in Wales. For example, mean intake of total fat was 81.7g for men in the Northern region compared with 90.1g for men in Central and South West regions of England and in Wales (p<0.05). Women in the Northern region had significantly lower mean daily intakes of *cis* monounsaturated fatty acids than those in London and the South East, 19.0g and 21.1g respectively (p<0.05).

Women in the Northern region derived a significantly lower proportion of their food energy from total fat, 33.9%, and from *cis* monounsaturated fatty acids, 11.0%, than women in London and the South East, 35.8% and 11.8% respectively (total fat: p<0.01; *cis* monounsaturated fatty acids: p<0.05). There were no significant regional differences for men in the proportion of food energy derived from total fat or fatty acids.

(Table 5.20)

5.9.2 Household receipt of benefits

Women in benefit households had a significantly lower mean daily intake of total fat, 56.4g, than those in non-benefit households, 62.5g (p<0.05)[7]. The same pattern is true for saturated and *cis* n-3 polyunsaturated fatty acids (p<0.01). There were no significant differences in mean intakes for men by household benefit status.

When intakes were expressed as a percentage of food energy, there were no significant differences in the fat and fatty acids composition of the diets of men and women from households receiving and not receiving benefits.

(Table 5.21)

Reference and Endnotes

1. Fat is a mixture of triglycerides (1 unit glycerol with 3 fatty acids), phospholipids, sterols and related compounds. Total fat includes all of these components.

2. Department of Health. Report on Health and Social Subjects 41. *Dietary Reference Values for Food Energy and Nutrients for the United Kingdom.* HMSO (London, 1991).

3. Department of Health. Report on Health and Social Subjects: 46. *Nutritional Aspects of Cardiovascular Disease.* HMSO (London, 1994).

4. For each sex and age group the distribution of data was evaluated using the skewness statistic in SPSS. If the skewness statistic was less than twice the standard error of the statistic then data were considered to be normally distributed.

5. Food and Agriculture Organisation. Food and Nutrition Paper: **57**. *Fats and Oils in Human Nutrition.* FAO (Rome, 1994).

6. The areas included in each of the four analysis 'regions' are given in the response chapter, Chapter 2 of the Technical Report, online at http://www.food.gov.uk/science. Definitions of 'regions' are given in the glossary (*see* Appendix C).

7. Households receiving benefits are those where someone in the respondent's household was currently receiving Working Families Tax Credit or had, in the previous 14 days, drawn Income Support or (Income-related) Job Seeker's Allowance. Definitions of 'household' and 'benefits (receiving)', are given in the glossary (*see* Appendix C).

Table 5.1

Average daily intake of total fat (g) by sex and age of respondent

Cumulative percentages

Average daily total fat intake (g)	Age (years):				All
	19–24	25–34	35–49	50–64	
	cum %	cum %	cum %	cum %	cum %
Men					
Less than 40	4	1	4	3	3
Less than 50	12	5	7	10	8
Less than 60	22	13	15	20	17
Less than 70	34	27	27	30	29
Less than 80	43	44	41	47	44
Less than 90	54	64	55	62	60
Less than 100	71	73	69	72	71
Less than 110	81	82	80	80	81
Less than 120	91	90	88	90	89
Less than 140	93	95	95	97	95
All	100	100	100	100	100
Base	*108*	*219*	*253*	*253*	*833*
Mean (average value)	85.8	87.1	88.3	84.5	86.5
Median	85.9	83.2	86.8	81.7	84.2
Lower 2.5 percentile	37.4	47.5	35.6	37.1	37.8
Upper 2.5 percentile	153.1	158.3	150.2	148.3	150.5
Standard deviation	29.23	28.02	28.95	27.08	28.17
	cum %	cum %	cum %	cum %	cum %
Women					
Less than 30	7	4	6	5	5
Less than 40	16	18	14	15	16
Less than 50	29	34	29	34	31
Less than 60	53	53	47	49	50
Less than 70	69	72	68	67	69
Less than 80	76	85	83	80	82
Less than 90	82	93	92	91	91
Less than 100	95	97	95	95	96
All	100	100	100	100	100
Base	*104*	*210*	*318*	*259*	*891*
Mean (average value)	63.9	59.8	61.9	61.2	61.4
Median	59.7	58.8	60.7	60.4	60.0
Lower 2.5 percentile	23.2	23.9	20.1	24.2	23.3
Upper 2.5 percentile	134.3	105.5	115.0	110.5	111.0
Standard deviation	26.44	19.74	21.45	21.50	21.72

Table 5.2

Percentage of food energy from total fat by sex and age of respondent

Cumulative percentages

Percentage of food energy from total fat	Age (years):				All
	19–24	25–34	35–49	50–64	
	cum %	cum %	cum %	cum %	cum %
Men					
25 or less	3	2	4	3	3
27 or less	7	4	8	8	7
30 or less	17	10	15	17	14
33 or less	28	27	27	32	29
35 or less	46	44	40	45	43
38 or less	65	66	63	63	64
40 or less	73	82	77	77	78
45 or less	93	97	96	97	96
All	100	100	100	100	100
Base	*108*	*219*	*253*	*253*	*833*
Mean (average value)	36.0	35.8	35.9	35.6	35.8
Median	35.7	35.5	36.2	36.0	36.0
Lower 2.5 percentile	21.6	26.0	23.2	23.9	24.0
Upper 2.5 percentile	46.7	47.2	46.0	46.1	46.6
Standard deviation	6.00	5.41	5.64	5.68	5.63
	cum %	cum %	cum %	cum %	cum %
Women					
25 or less	5	4	8	8	7
27 or less	10	8	12	15	12
30 or less	23	19	22	23	22
33 or less	37	30	34	43	36
35 or less	49	45	49	56	50
38 or less	66	68	70	69	69
40 or less	83	77	82	79	80
42 or less	95	96	96	93	95
All	100	100	100	100	100
Base	*104*	*210*	*318*	*259*	*891*
Mean (average value)	35.5	35.4	34.7	34.5	34.9
Median	35.3	35.6	35.2	34.0	34.7
Lower 2.5 percentile	24.0	22.3	20.8	22.4	22.0
Upper 2.5 percentile	51.1	46.1	46.1	47.8	47.9
Standard deviation	7.58	5.90	6.33	6.77	6.52

Table 5.3

Average daily intake of saturated fatty acids (g) by sex and age of respondent

Cumulative percentages

Average daily saturated fatty acids intake (g)	Age (years):				All
	19–24	25–34	35–49	50–64	
	cum %	cum %	cum %	cum %	cum %
Men					
Less than 15	5	3	5	5	4
Less than 20	15	10	13	15	13
Less than 25	28	27	25	29	27
Less than 30	45	47	44	48	46
Less than 35	63	69	57	61	62
Less than 40	78	81	74	76	77
Less than 45	85	87	86	88	87
Less than 50	94	92	92	94	93
Less than 55	96	94	94	96	95
Less than 60	98	97	97	97	97
All	100	100	100	100	100
Base	*108*	*219*	*253*	*253*	*833*
Mean (average value)	32.3	32.2	33.4	32.0	32.5
Median	31.7	30.7	32.6	30.4	31.0
Lower 2.5 percentile	12.1	14.9	12.4	12.4	12.9
Upper 2.5 percentile	61.9	62.4	62.0	62.7	62.3
Standard deviation	12.19	11.93	12.54	11.92	12.14
	cum %	cum %	cum %	cum %	cum %
Women					
Less than 10	5	2	6	4	5
Less than 15	17	22	17	19	18
Less than 20	46	42	34	42	40
Less than 25	68	62	59	60	61
Less than 30	82	84	79	75	80
Less than 35	89	92	90	87	90
Less than 40	92	96	95	94	94
Less than 45	95	99	97	98	98
All	100	100	100	100	100
Base	*104*	*210*	*318*	*259*	*891*
Mean (average value)	23.5	22.4	23.6	23.7	23.3
Median	21.1	22.2	22.5	22.2	22.2
Lower 2.5 percentile	7.3	8.9	7.6	7.7	7.9
Upper 2.5 percentile	64.6	40.6	45.3	46.1	44.9
Standard deviation	11.93	8.27	9.29	9.86	9.57

Table 5.4

Percentage of food energy from saturated fatty acids by sex and age of respondent

Cumulative percentages

Percentage of food energy from saturated fatty acids	Age (years):				All
	19–24	25–34	35–49	50–64	
	cum %	cum %	cum %	cum %	cum %
Men					
8 or less	3	2	3	3	3
10 or less	14	8	12	13	12
12 or less	22	36	26	36	31
14 or less	60	60	59	58	59
16 or less	81	88	82	80	83
18 or less	91	97	94	93	94
20 or less	98	100	98	98	98
All	100		100	100	100
Base	*108*	*219*	*253*	*253*	*833*
Mean (average value)	13.5	13.2	13.5	13.4	13.4
Median	13.1	13.4	13.5	13.3	13.4
Lower 2.5 percentile	7.2	8.5	7.2	7.7	7.8
Upper 2.5 percentile	19.4	18.3	19.1	20.3	19.0
Standard deviation	3.00	2.58	2.99	3.13	2.93
	cum %	cum %	cum %	cum %	cum %
Women					
8 or less	4	4	7	6	6
10 or less	18	16	16	20	17
12 or less	44	32	33	36	35
14 or less	71	55	61	62	61
16 or less	88	85	83	80	83
18 or less	95	95	95	89	93
20 or less	97	100	98	95	98
All	100		100	100	100
Base	*104*	*210*	*318*	*259*	*891*
Mean (average value)	12.9	13.2	13.2	13.3	13.2
Median	12.7	13.4	13.3	13.0	13.1
Lower 2.5 percentile	7.4	7.5	7.1	6.6	7.2
Upper 2.5 percentile	25.5	18.6	19.7	21.1	20.0
Standard deviation	3.97	2.86	3.10	3.65	3.32

Table 5.5

Average daily intake of *trans* fatty acids (g) by sex and age of respondent

Cumulative percentages

Average daily *trans* fatty acids intake (g)	Age (years):				All
	19–24	25–34	35–49	50–64	
	cum %	cum %	cum %	cum %	cum %
Men					
Less than 1.00	5	2	5	4	4
Less than 2.00	20	27	28	28	27
Less than 3.00	59	66	58	60	61
Less than 4.00	81	84	80	83	82
Less than 5.00	93	91	92	94	92
Less than 6.00	98	96	95	98	97
All	100	100	100	100	100
Base	*108*	*219*	*253*	*253*	*833*
Mean (average value)	2.95	2.86	2.98	2.86	2.91
Median	2.72	2.57	2.65	2.62	2.63
Lower 2.5 percentile	0.84	1.02	0.79	0.78	0.83
Upper 2.5 percentile	6.05	6.77	6.80	5.83	6.71
Standard deviation	1.283	1.405	1.606	1.390	1.450
	cum %	cum %	cum %	cum %	cum %
Women					
Less than 0.50	1	1	1	3	2
Less than 1.00	12	14	15	14	14
Less than 2.00	60	55	52	52	54
Less than 3.00	87	89	84	79	84
Less than 4.00	96	98	96	93	96
Less than 5.00	97	100	99	98	99
All	100		100	100	100
Base	*104*	*210*	*318*	*259*	*891*
Mean (average value)	2.00	1.93	2.06	2.12	2.04
Median	1.71	1.83	1.93	1.95	1.89
Lower 2.5 percentile	0.65	0.58	0.57	0.48	0.56
Upper 2.5 percentile	5.70	4.03	4.30	4.54	4.37
Standard deviation	1.114	0.866	0.983	1.110	1.013

Table 5.6

Percentage of food energy from *trans* fatty acids by sex and age of respondent

Cumulative percentages

Percentage of food energy from *trans* fatty acids	Age (years):				All
	19–24	25–34	35–49	50–64	
	cum %	cum %	cum %	cum %	cum %
Men					
0.5 or less	2	2	4	2	2
0.7 or less	7	9	11	10	10
1.0 or less	29	38	38	35	36
1.3 or less	66	70	65	64	66
1.6 or less	83	87	84	90	87
1.9 or less	97	95	93	95	95
2.2 or less	99	99	97	98	98
All	100	100	100	100	100
Base	*108*	*219*	*253*	*253*	*833*
Mean (average value)	1.2	1.2	1.2	1.2	1.2
Median	1.2	1.1	1.1	1.2	1.2
Lower 2.5 percentile	0.5	0.6	0.4	0.5	0.5
Upper 2.5 percentile	1.9	2.0	2.3	2.1	2.1
Standard deviation	0.44	0.38	0.46	0.42	0.43
	cum %	cum %	cum %	cum %	cum %
Women					
0.5 or less	1	4	5	5	4
0.7 or less	14	10	14	16	14
1.0 or less	42	37	38	38	38
1.3 or less	75	73	67	64	68
1.6 or less	88	90	87	82	86
1.9 or less	96	97	95	94	96
2.2 or less	97	99	98	98	98
All	100	100	100	100	100
Base	*104*	*210*	*318*	*259*	*891*
Mean (average value)	1.1	1.1	1.2	1.2	1.2
Median	1.1	1.1	1.1	1.1	1.1
Lower 2.5 percentile	0.6	0.4	0.5	0.4	0.4
Upper 2.5 percentile	2.2	2.1	2.1	2.1	2.1
Standard deviation	0.41	0.39	0.42	0.45	0.42

Table 5.7

Average daily intake of *cis* monounsaturated fatty acids (g) by sex and age of respondent

Cumulative percentages

Average daily intake of *cis* monounsaturated fatty acids (g)	Age (years):				All
	19–24	25–34	35–49	50–64	
	cum %	cum %	cum %	cum %	cum %
Men					
Less than 12	3	0	3	3	2
Less than 16	6	5	7	8	7
Less than 20	21	11	15	21	17
Less than 24	30	29	31	35	32
Less than 28	42	48	48	54	49
Less than 32	64	64	65	71	66
Less than 36	71	78	75	80	77
Less than 40	88	86	86	90	88
Less than 44	91	92	92	96	93
All	100	100	100	100	100
Base	*108*	*219*	*253*	*253*	*833*
Mean (average value)	29.6	29.9	29.6	27.9	29.1
Median	29.5	28.4	28.6	27.0	28.2
Lower 2.5 percentile	9.9	15.2	11.6	11.6	12.9
Upper 2.5 percentile	53.5	52.9	50.5	47.2	51.0
Standard deviation	10.46	9.50	10.12	9.23	9.76
	cum %	cum %	cum %	cum %	cum %
Women					
Less than 8	1	2	5	3	3
Less than 12	12	12	12	10	12
Less than 16	24	32	28	35	30
Less than 20	48	53	51	54	52
Less than 24	68	74	73	75	73
Less than 28	76	88	88	89	87
Less than 32	84	96	93	94	93
Less than 36	95	98	97	98	97
Less than 40	97	100	99	99	99
All	100		100	100	100
Base	*104*	*210*	*318*	*259*	*891*
Mean (average value)	21.8	19.9	20.2	19.7	20.2
Median	20.5	19.4	19.9	18.9	19.7
Lower 2.5 percentile	8.1	7.6	6.6	7.2	7.2
Upper 2.5 percentile	41.6	35.5	36.4	36.0	36.7
Standard deviation	8.77	6.88	7.30	7.23	7.39

Table 5.8

Percentage of food energy from *cis* monounsaturated fatty acids by sex and age of respondent

Cumulative percentages

Percentage of food energy from *cis* monounsaturated fatty acids	Age (years):				All
	19–24	25–34	35–49	50–64	
	cum %	cum %	cum %	cum %	cum %
Men					
7.5 or less	2	1	4	3	3
10.5 or less	21	18	26	31	25
11.5 or less	37	32	41	44	39
12.5 or less	44	54	55	62	56
13.5 or less	69	74	75	74	74
14.5 or less	82	85	85	90	86
15.5 or less	88	94	94	96	94
16.5 or less	96	97	98	98	98
All	100	100	100	100	100
Base	*108*	*219*	*253*	*253*	*833*
Mean (average value)	12.4	12.3	12.0	11.8	12.1
Median	12.8	12.3	12.2	11.7	12.1
Lower 2.5 percentile	6.9	8.7	7.4	7.4	7.5
Upper 2.5 percentile	16.6	16.7	16.5	16.3	16.5
Standard deviation	2.36	2.21	2.29	2.30	2.29
	cum %	cum %	cum %	cum %	cum %
Women					
7.5 or less	2	3	8	7	6
10.5 or less	29	31	35	43	36
11.5 or less	40	50	51	57	51
12.5 or less	59	65	67	73	67
13.5 or less	73	76	79	87	80
14.5 or less	81	91	89	90	89
15.5 or less	90	94	96	94	94
16.5 or less	95	97	99	97	97
All	100	100	100	100	100
Base	*104*	*210*	*318*	*259*	*891*
Mean (average value)	12.2	11.7	11.3	11.1	11.5
Median	12.1	11.6	11.4	11.2	11.4
Lower 2.5 percentile	7.5	7.5	5.7	6.4	6.7
Upper 2.5 percentile	17.3	16.9	15.9	17.3	16.7
Standard deviation	2.87	2.40	2.56	2.57	2.58

Table 5.9

Average daily intake of *cis* n–3 polyunsaturated fatty acids (g) by sex and age of respondent

Cumulative percentages

Average daily *cis* n–3 polyunsaturated fatty acids intake (g)	Age (years):				All
	19–24	25–34	35–49	50–64	
	cum %	cum %	cum %	cum %	cum %
Men					
Less than 0.70	1	1	2	2	1
Less than 1.00	4	3	4	5	4
Less than 1.50	20	16	16	20	18
Less than 2.00	54	45	43	43	45
Less than 2.50	74	70	65	65	67
Less than 3.00	82	86	83	80	82
Less than 3.50	96	92	89	90	91
Less than 4.00	97	95	95	95	95
Less than 4.50	100	97	98	97	98
All		100	100	100	100
Base	*108*	*219*	*253*	*253*	*833*
Mean (average value)	2.10	2.30	2.31	2.29	2.27
Median	1.95	2.08	2.13	2.18	2.09
Lower 2.5 percentile	0.89	0.99	0.86	0.81	0.88
Upper 2.5 percentile	4.25	5.22	4.46	4.71	4.40
Standard deviation	0.750	1.100	0.920	0.960	0.960
	cum %	cum %	cum %	cum %	cum %
Women					
Less than 0.70	1	3	5	3	4
Less than 1.00	17	12	13	10	12
Less than 1.50	44	51	49	42	47
Less than 2.00	71	78	71	65	71
Less than 2.50	92	90	87	84	88
Less than 3.00	94	97	96	90	95
Less than 3.50	98	99	98	97	98
All	100	100	100	100	100
Base	*104*	*210*	*318*	*259*	*891*
Mean (average value)	1.69	1.60	1.68	1.82	1.71
Median	1.59	1.49	1.52	1.63	1.55
Lower 2.5 percentile	0.73	0.67	0.59	0.66	0.63
Upper 2.5 percentile	3.41	3.14	3.44	3.59	3.41
Standard deviation	0.750	0.630	0.760	0.880	0.770

Table 5.10

Average daily intake of *cis* n–6 polyunsaturated fatty acids (g) by sex and age of respondent

Cumulative percentages

Average daily *cis* n–6 polyunsaturated fatty acids intake (g)	Age (years):				All
	19–24	25–34	35–49	50–64	
	cum %	cum %	cum %	cum %	cum %
Men					
Less than 6.0	4	4	5	8	5
Less than 8.0	14	9	12	20	14
Less than 10.0	32	27	26	36	30
Less than 12.0	54	44	47	51	48
Less than 14.0	67	64	61	69	65
Less than 16.0	83	80	78	77	79
Less than 18.0	87	89	87	84	87
Less than 20.0	94	94	92	92	93
All	100	100	100	100	100
Base	*108*	*219*	*253*	*253*	*833*
Mean (average value)	12.6	13.1	13.1	12.6	12.9
Median	11.4	12.6	12.5	11.8	12.3
Lower 2.5 percentile	4.9	5.4	4.8	4.5	4.9
Upper 2.5 percentile	25.4	25.8	25.6	23.9	25.4
Standard deviation	5.35	4.59	4.91	6.09	5.27
	cum %	cum %	cum %	cum %	cum %
Women					
Less than 4.0	4	4	4	5	4
Less than 6.0	16	18	18	24	20
Less than 8.0	36	42	40	45	41
Less than 10.0	59	63	61	63	62
Less than 12.0	74	80	76	83	79
Less than 14.0	86	91	86	90	88
Less than 16.0	90	93	92	98	94
Less than 18.0	92	94	97	99	96
All	100	100	100	100	100
Base	*104*	*210*	*318*	*259*	*891*
Mean (average value)	10.1	9.4	9.5	8.8	9.4
Median	9.3	8.8	9.1	8.5	8.9
Lower 2.5 percentile	3.7	3.4	3.3	3.1	4.0
Upper 2.5 percentile	21.8	20.5	18.0	16.1	18.7
Standard deviation	4.95	3.95	3.91	3.54	3.33

Table 5.11

Percentage of food energy from *cis* n–3 polyunsaturated fatty acids by sex and age of respondent

Cumulative percentages

Percentage of food energy from *cis* n–3 polyunsaturated fatty acids	Age (years):				All
	19–24	25–34	35–49	50–64	
	cum %	cum %	cum %	cum %	cum %
Men					
0.4 or less	–	1	1	1	1
0.6 or less	11	10	8	12	10
0.8 or less	36	36	37	37	37
1.0 or less	78	67	65	61	66
1.2 or less	86	83	83	78	82
1.4 or less	96	92	93	91	92
1.6 or less	98	95	96	94	95
All	100	100	100	100	100
Base	*108*	*219*	*253*	*253*	*833*
Mean (average value)	0.9	1.0	1.0	1.0	1.0
Median	0.9	0.9	0.9	0.9	0.9
Lower 2.5 percentile	0.5	0.5	0.5	0.5	0.5
Upper 2.5 percentile	1.6	2.3	1.9	2.1	1.9
Standard deviation	0.26	0.42	0.35	0.39	0.37
	cum %	cum %	cum %	cum %	cum %
Women					
0.4 or less	–	–	2	1	1
0.6 or less	5	9	11	9	9
0.8 or less	34	36	37	33	35
1.0 or less	66	61	64	55	61
1.2 or less	86	82	79	74	79
1.4 or less	90	92	89	85	89
1.6 or less	95	96	95	89	93
All	100	100	100	100	100
Base	*104*	*210*	*318*	*259*	*891*
Mean (average value)	1.0	1.0	1.0	1.1	1.0
Median	0.9	0.9	0.9	0.9	0.9
Lower 2.5 percentile	0.6	0.5	0.4	0.5	0.5
Upper 2.5 percentile	1.7	1.9	1.8	2.3	2.0
Standard deviation	0.35	0.33	0.41	0.59	0.45

Table 5.12

Percentage of food energy from *cis* n–6 polyunsaturated fatty acids by sex and age of respondent

Cumulative percentages

Percentage of food energy from *cis* n–6 polyunsaturated fatty acids	Age (years):				All
	19–24	25–34	35–49	50–64	
	cum %	cum %	cum %	cum %	cum %
Men					
3.0 or less	1	2	3	6	3
4.0 or less	20	17	16	25	20
5.0 or less	44	40	42	52	45
6.0 or less	74	67	70	72	71
7.0 or less	89	90	91	83	88
8.0 or less	96	98	94	94	95
All	100	100	100	100	100
Base	*108*	*219*	*253*	*253*	*833*
Mean (average value)	5.3	5.4	5.4	5.3	5.4
Median	5.1	5.5	5.3	5.0	5.1
Lower 2.5 percentile	3.3	3.3	2.9	2.7	2.8
Upper 2.5 percentile	9.3	8.0	8.5	9.0	8.7
Standard deviation	1.45	1.33	1.45	1.87	1.56
	cum %	cum %	cum %	cum %	cum %
Women					
3.0 or less	–	4	4	7	4
4.0 or less	14	15	21	28	21
5.0 or less	36	41	46	54	46
6.0 or less	62	66	72	77	71
7.0 or less	82	87	83	89	86
8.0 or less	94	93	93	97	94
All	100	100	100	100	100
Base	*104*	*210*	*318*	*259*	*891*
Mean (average value)	5.6	5.6	5.3	5.0	5.3
Median	5.2	5.5	5.1	4.9	5.1
Lower 2.5 percentile	3.5	2.9	2.8	2.5	2.7
Upper 2.5 percentile	8.3	9.9	9.0	8.1	8.8
Standard deviation	1.67	1.76	1.62	1.49	1.64

Table 5.13

Average daily intake of cholesterol (mg) by sex and age of respondent

Cumulative percentages

Average daily cholesterol intake (mg)	Age (years):				All
	19–24	25–34	35–49	50–64	
	cum %	cum %	cum %	cum %	cum %
Men					
Less than 100	7	2	3	2	3
Less than 150	17	8	8	5	8
Less than 200	30	19	18	14	19
Less than 250	56	37	37	34	38
Less than 300	69	56	54	53	56
Less than 350	75	74	68	65	70
Less than 400	82	85	79	76	80
Less than 450	87	90	86	86	87
Less than 500	95	94	92	90	92
All	100	100	100	100	100
Base	*108*	*219*	*253*	*253*	*833*
Mean (average value)	269	298	309	319	304
Median	237	284	293	292	285
Lower 2.5 percentile	74	120	99	108	95
Upper 2.5 percentile	627	604	604	663	606
Standard deviation	133.7	120.3	129.6	127.0	127.7
	cum %	cum %	cum %	cum %	cum %
Women					
Less than 100	14	16	7	2	9
Less than 150	43	35	24	15	26
Less than 200	60	63	47	39	50
Less than 250	73	79	72	60	70
Less than 300	88	89	83	77	83
Less than 350	94	95	94	88	92
Less than 400	95	98	97	93	96
All	100	100	100	100	100
Base	*104*	*210*	*318*	*259*	*891*
Mean (average value)	196	188	214	239	213
Median	174	178	209	223	201
Lower 2.5 percentile	41	59	57	100	60
Upper 2.5 percentile	465	397	423	452	427
Standard deviation	111.8	82.5	92.1	92.6	94.5

Table 5.14

Percentage contribution of food types to average daily intake of total fat by sex and age of respondent

Percentages

Type of food	Men aged (years):				All men	Women aged (years):				All women	All
	19–24	25–34	35–49	50–64		19–24	25–34	35–49	50–64		
	%	%	%	%	%	%	%	%	%	%	%
Cereals & cereal products	18	19	19	19	19	18	20	19	20	20	19
of which:											
pizza	4	2	1	1	2	3	2	1	1	2	2
white bread	2	2	2	2	2	4	2	2	2	2	2
biscuits	2	3	4	4	3	2	3	4	4	3	3
buns, cakes & pastries	3	3	4	5	4	2	4	4	5	4	4
Milk & milk products	9	13	14	15	14	13	15	15	16	15	14
of which:											
whole milk	1	3	3	2	2	3	3	3	2	3	3
semi–skimmed milk	2	2	3	3	3	2	3	3	3	3	3
cheese (incl. cottage cheese)	5	6	6	6	6	5	7	6	6	6	6
Eggs & egg dishes	4	4	4	5	4	3	3	4	5	4	4
Fat spreads	13	10	12	14	12	9	10	11	12	11	12
of which:											
butter	3	2	4	5	3	2	3	4	5	4	4
margarines	2	2	2	1	2	1	1	1	1	1	1
reduced fat spreads (60–80% fat)	6	6	5	6	6	5	4	5	5	5	5
low fat spreads (40% fat or less)	1	1	1	1	1	1	1	1	1	1	1
Meat & meat products	29	26	25	23	25	24	19	20	19	20	23
of which:											
bacon & ham	3	2	3	3	3	2	2	2	2	2	2
beef, veal & dishes	4	3	3	3	3	4	3	3	3	3	3
lamb & dishes	1	1	1	1	1	1	1	1	1	1	1
pork & dishes	1	1	1	1	1	1	1	1	1	1	1
coated chicken & turkey	2	2	1	1	1	2	2	2	1	1	1
chicken, turkey & dishes	4	4	4	3	4	4	4	4	3	4	4
burgers & kebabs	5	3	2	0	2	3	2	1	0	1	2
sausages	4	3	3	3	3	3	2	2	2	2	3
meat pies & pastries	4	4	4	5	4	3	3	3	3	3	4
other meat & meat products	1	1	1	2	1	1	0	1	1	1	1
Fish & fish dishes	2	2	3	4	3	2	3	4	6	4	3
of which:											
coated &/or fried white fish	1	1	1	2	2	1	1	2	2	2	2
oily fish	0	1	1	2	1	1	1	2	3	2	1
Vegetables (excluding potatoes)	2	4	4	4	4	4	7	5	4	5	4
Potatoes & savoury snacks	15	11	9	7	10	16	12	9	7	10	10
of which:											
chips	8	5	5	4	5	8	5	4	3	5	5
other fried or roast potatoes	1	1	1	1	1	1	1	1	1	1	1
savoury snacks	5	4	3	2	3	6	5	3	1	3	3
Fruit & nuts	0	2	2	2	2	2	2	2	2	2	2
Sugar, preserves & confectionery	5	4	3	2	3	4	4	4	3	4	3
of which:											
chocolate confectionery	4	3	3	2	3	4	4	4	3	4	3
Drinks*	0	0	0	0	0	0	0	0	0	0	0
Miscellaneous**	3	4	4	4	4	5	6	6	5	5	5
Average daily intake (g)	85.8	87.1	88.3	84.5	86.5	63.9	59.8	61.9	61.2	61.4	73.5
Total number of respondents	108	219	253	253	833	104	210	318	259	891	1724

Note: * Includes soft drinks, alcoholic drinks, tea, coffee and water.

** Includes powdered beverages (except tea and coffee), soups, sauces, condiments and artificial sweeteners.

Table 5.15

Percentage contribution of food types to average daily intake of saturated fatty acids by sex and age of respondent

Percentages

Type of food	Men aged (years):				All men	Women aged (years):				All women	All
	19–24	25–34	35–49	50–64		19–24	25–34	35–49	50–64		
	%	%	%	%	%	%	%	%	%	%	%
Cereals & cereal products	17	18	17	18	17	18	19	18	19	19	18
of which:											
pizza	5	3	2	1	2	3	3	1	1	2	2
white bread	1	1	1	1	1	5	1	1	1	2	1
biscuits	3	4	4	4	4	3	3	4	4	4	4
buns, cakes & pastries	3	3	4	5	4	2	4	4	5	4	4
Milk & milk products	16	22	24	25	23	22	25	25	26	25	24
of which:											
whole milk	1	4	4	4	4	5	5	5	4	4	4
semi–skimmed milk	3	4	5	5	4	3	4	5	6	5	5
cheese (incl. cottage cheese)	8	10	10	11	10	9	11	9	10	10	10
Eggs & egg dishes	3	3	3	4	3	3	3	3	4	3	3
Fat spreads	12	9	11	14	12	8	9	11	13	11	11
of which:											
butter	6	3	6	8	6	3	5	6	8	6	6
margarines	2	1	1	1	1	1	1	1	1	1	1
polyunsaturated reduced fat spreads (60–80% fat)	1	1	1	2	1	0	1	1	1	1	1
other reduced fat spreads (60–80% fat)	3	3	2	2	2	3	2	2	2	2	2
low fat spreads (40% fat or less)	0	1	1	1	1	0	1	1	1	1	1
Meat & meat products	29	26	25	23	25	24	18	19	18	19	22
of which:											
bacon & ham	3	2	2	3	3	2	2	2	2	2	2
beef, veal & dishes	5	4	4	4	4	4	3	4	4	4	4
lamb & dishes	1	1	1	2	1	1	1	1	2	1	1
pork & dishes	1	1	1	1	1	1	1	1	1	1	1
coated chicken & turkey	2	1	1	0	1	2	1	1	1	1	1
chicken, turkey & dishes	2	3	3	2	3	3	3	3	2	3	3
burgers & kebabs	6	4	2	0	3	4	2	1	0	2	2
sausages	4	3	3	2	3	2	2	2	2	2	3
meat pies & pastries	5	5	4	5	5	3	3	3	3	3	4
other meat & meat products	1	1	1	2	1	1	0	1	1	1	1
Fish & fish dishes	1	1	2	3	2	1	2	2	3	2	2
of which:											
coated &/or fried white fish	1	1	1	1	1	1	1	1	1	1	1
oily fish	0	1	1	1	1	0	1	1	2	1	1
Vegetables (excluding potatoes)	1	2	2	2	2	2	4	3	2	3	2
Potatoes & savoury snacks	11	8	7	5	7	12	9	7	5	7	7
of which:											
chips	5	3	3	2	3	4	3	3	2	3	3
other fried or roast potatoes	0	0	0	1	0	0	0	0	1	0	0
savoury snacks	5	4	3	2	3	6	5	3	1	3	3
Fruit & nuts	0	1	1	1	1	1	1	2	1	1	1
Sugar, preserves & confectionery	7	2	4	3	4	6	6	6	4	5	5
of which:											
chocolate confectionery	6	2	4	3	4	6	6	5	4	5	5
Drinks*	1	1	1	1	1	0	1	1	0	1	1
Miscellaneous**	2	3	3	3	3	3	4	4	3	3	3
Average daily intake (g)	**32.3**	**32.2**	**33.4**	**32.0**	**32.5**	**23.5**	**22.4**	**23.6**	**23.7**	**23.3**	**27.8**
Total number of respondents	**108**	**219**	**253**	**253**	**833**	**104**	**210**	**318**	**259**	**891**	**1724**

Note: * *Includes soft drinks, alcoholic drinks, tea, coffee and water.*

** *Includes powdered beverages (except tea and coffee), soups, sauces, condiments and artificial sweeteners.*

Table 5.16

Percentage contribution of food types to average daily intake of *trans* fatty acids by sex and age of respondent

Percentages

Type of food	Men aged (years):				All men	Women aged (years):				All women	All
	19–24	25–34	35–49	50–64		19–24	25–34	35–49	50–64		
	%	%	%	%	%	%	%	%	%	%	%
Cereals & cereal products	20	25	26	27	25	21	25	26	30	26	26
of which:											
pizza	3	2	1	1	1	2	2	1	0	1	1
white bread	1	1	1	1	1	4	1	1	1	1	1
biscuits	6	9	10	9	9	6	7	9	9	8	9
buns, cakes & pastries	5	6	7	10	8	4	9	9	11	9	8
puddings	1	1	2	2	2	1	2	2	2	2	2
Milk & milk products	10	14	15	16	15	15	17	15	17	16	16
of which:											
whole milk	0	1	1	1	1	2	2	1	1	1	1
semi–skimmed milk	2	3	4	3	3	2	4	4	4	4	4
cheese (incl. cottage cheese)	6	8	7	8	8	7	8	7	7	7	8
ice cream	1	1	1	1	1	2	2	1	2	1	1
Eggs & egg dishes	2	2	2	3	2	2	3	3	3	3	3
Fat spreads	21	16	19	20	19	19	14	18	19	17	18
of which:											
butter	4	2	4	5	4	2	3	4	6	4	4
margarines	6	5	5	4	5	4	4	5	4	4	5
polyunsaturated reduced fat spreads (60–80% fat)	1	0	1	2	1	1	1	0	1	0	1
other reduced fat spreads (60–80% fat)	9	7	8	6	7	12	5	7	7	7	7
low fat spreads (40% fat or less)	1	1	1	2	2	1	2	2	2	1	2
Meat & meat products	26	25	22	20	23	24	18	17	16	18	21
of which:											
bacon & ham	0	0	0	0	0	1	1	0	0	0	0
beef, veal & dishes	4	4	4	4	4	5	4	4	4	4	4
lamb & dishes	2	2	2	3	2	2	2	2	3	2	2
pork & dishes	0	0	0	0	0	0	0	0	0	0	0
coated chicken & turkey	2	1	1	0	1	2	1	1	0	1	1
chicken, turkey & dishes	1	2	2	1	1	2	2	1	1	1	1
burgers & kebabs	5	4	3	1	3	4	3	1	0	2	2
sausages	1	1	1	1	1	1	1	0	0	0	1
meat pies & pastries	9	9	8	8	9	7	6	5	5	5	7
other meat & meat products	1	1	1	1	1	1	1	0	1	0	1
Fish & fish dishes	2	2	2	3	3	2	2	3	3	3	3
of which:											
coated &/or fried white fish	2	2	2	2	2	2	2	2	2	2	2
Vegetables (excluding potatoes)	1	1	1	0	1	2	3	2	1	1	1
Potatoes & savoury snacks	8	7	6	5	7	9	9	6	4	6	6
of which:											
chips	6	5	4	3	4	6	5	4	3	4	4
other fried or roast potatoes	0	0	0	0	0	0	0	0	0	0	0
savoury snacks	2	1	1	1	1	2	3	1	0	1	1
Fruit & nuts	0	0	0	0	0	0	0	0	0	0	0
Sugar, preserves & confectionery	6	4	4	2	4	5	4	4	3	4	4
of which:											
chocolate confectionery	6	4	4	2	3	4	4	3	2	3	3
Drinks*	0	1	0	0	0	0	0	0	0	0	0
Miscellaneous**	2	2	2	2	2	3	3	3	3	3	3
Average daily intake (g)	**2.95**	**2.86**	**2.98**	**2.86**	**2.91**	**2.00**	**1.93**	**2.06**	**2.12**	**2.04**	**2.46**
Total number of respondents	**108**	**219**	**253**	**253**	**833**	**104**	**210**	**318**	**259**	**891**	**1724**

Note: *   Includes soft drinks, alcoholic drinks, tea, coffee and water.

** Includes powdered beverages (except tea and coffee), soups, sauces, condiments and artificial sweeteners.

Table 5.17

Percentage contribution of food types to average daily intake of *cis* monounsaturated fatty acids by sex and age of respondent

Percentages

Type of food	Men aged (years):				All men	Women aged (years):				All women	All
	19–24	25–34	35–49	50–64		19–24	25–34	35–49	50–64		
	%	%	%	%	%	%	%	%	%	%	%
Cereals & cereal products	17	17	17	17	17	15	18	18	18	18	17
of which:											
pizza	4	2	1	1	2	2	2	1	1	2	2
white bread	1	1	2	1	2	3	1	1	1	1	2
biscuits	2	3	3	3	3	2	2	3	3	3	3
buns, cakes & pastries	3	3	4	5	4	1	4	4	5	4	4
Milk & milk products	6	9	10	11	9	9	11	11	12	11	10
of which:											
whole milk	1	2	2	2	2	2	2	2	2	2	2
semi-skimmed milk	1	2	2	2	2	1	2	2	2	2	2
cheese (incl. cottage cheese)	3	4	4	5	4	4	5	4	4	4	4
Eggs & egg dishes	4	5	4	6	5	4	4	5	5	5	5
Fat spreads	12	11	11	13	12	9	9	11	12	11	11
of which:											
butter	2	1	2	3	2	1	2	2	4	3	2
margarines	2	2	2	2	2	1	1	2	2	1	2
polyunsaturated reduced fat spreads (60-80% fat)	1	1	1	2	1	0	1	1	1	1	1
other reduced fat spreads (60-80% fat)	5	5	4	4	5	6	3	5	4	4	4
low fat spreads (40% fat or less)	0	1	1	1	1	0	1	1	1	1	1
Meat & meat products	33	30	30	28	30	27	22	24	24	24	27
of which:											
bacon & ham	4	3	3	4	3	2	2	2	3	2	3
beef, veal & dishes	4	4	4	4	4	5	3	4	4	4	4
lamb & dishes	1	1	1	1	1	1	1	1	1	1	1
pork & dishes	1	1	2	2	1	1	1	1	1	1	1
coated chicken & turkey	2	2	2	1	1	3	2	2	1	2	2
chicken, turkey & dishes	5	5	5	4	5	5	5	5	5	5	5
burgers & kebabs	5	3	2	1	2	4	2	1	1	2	2
sausages	6	4	4	3	4	3	3	3	3	3	3
meat pies & pastries	5	5	5	5	5	3	3	4	3	3	4
other meat & meat products	1	1	2	2	2	1	1	1	2	1	1
Fish & fish dishes	2	2	3	5	3	2	3	4	6	4	4
of which:											
coated &/or fried white fish	1	1	2	2	2	1	1	2	2	2	2
oily fish	0	1	2	2	1	1	1	2	4	2	2
Vegetables (excluding potatoes)	2	4	4	4	4	4	8	5	4	5	4
Potatoes & savoury snacks	17	12	11	9	11	19	14	11	8	12	12
of which:											
chips	10	6	6	5	6	10	7	5	4	6	6
other fried or roast potatoes	1	1	1	1	1	1	1	1	1	1	1
savoury snacks	6	4	3	2	4	6	5	4	2	4	4
Fruit & nuts	0	2	2	2	2	2	2	2	3	3	2
Sugar, preserves & confectionery	4	4	3	2	3	4	4	4	3	4	3
of which:											
chocolate confectionery	4	3	3	2	3	3	4	4	3	3	3
Drinks*	0	0	0	0	0	0	0	0	0	0	0
Miscellaneous**	3	3	4	4	4	4	5	5	4	4	4
Average daily intake (g)	**29.6**	**29.9**	**29.6**	**27.9**	**29.1**	**21.8**	**19.9**	**20.2**	**19.7**	**20.2**	**24.5**
Total number of respondents	**108**	**219**	**253**	**253**	**833**	**104**	**210**	**318**	**259**	**891**	**1724**

*Note: * Includes soft drinks, alcoholic drinks, tea, coffee and water.*

*** Includes powdered beverages (except tea and coffee), soups, sauces, condiments and artificial sweeteners.*

Table 5.18

Percentage contribution of food types to average daily intake of *cis* n-3 polyunsaturated fatty acids by sex and age of respondent

Percentage

Type of food	Men aged (years):				All men	Women aged (years):				All women	All
	19–24	25–34	35–49	50–64		19–24	25–34	35–49	50–64		
	%	%	%	%	%	%	%	%	%	%	%
Cereals & cereal products	20	18	17	16	17	20	19	16	14	16	17
of which:											
pizza	5	3	2	1	2	3	3	2	1	2	2
white bread	3	3	3	3	3	4	2	2	2	2	3
buns, cakes & pastries	2	2	2	3	2	1	2	2	2	2	2
Milk & milk products	3	4	4	4	4	4	4	4	4	4	4
of which:											
cheese (incl. cottage cheese)	2	2	2	2	2	2	2	2	2	2	2
Eggs & egg dishes	2	3	2	3	3	2	2	2	2	2	2
Fat spreads	7	7	8	7	7	6	5	7	6	6	7
of which:											
butter	1	1	1	2	1	1	1	1	2	1	1
margarines	3	2	2	2	2	1	1	2	2	1	2
polyunsaturated reduced fat spreads (60-80% fat)	0	0	0	0	0	0	0	0	0	0	0
other reduced fat spreads (60-80% fat)	2	4	4	3	3	4	2	3	2	3	3
low fat spreads (40% fat or less)	0	1	0	1	1	0	1	1	1	1	1
Meat & meat products	24	19	19	15	19	17	15	15	13	14	17
of which:											
bacon & ham	2	1	2	2	2	1	1	1	1	1	1
beef, veal & dishes	2	2	2	2	2	2	2	2	1	2	2
lamb & dishes	1	1	1	1	1	0	0	1	1	1	1
pork & dishes	1	1	1	1	1	1	1	1	1	1	1
coated chicken & turkey	2	2	2	1	1	3	2	2	1	2	2
chicken, turkey & dishes	6	6	6	4	6	6	5	5	4	5	5
burgers & kebabs	4	2	1	0	1	2	1	1	0	1	1
sausages	3	2	2	1	2	1	1	1	1	1	1
meat pies & pastries	2	2	2	2	2	1	1	1	1	1	2
other meat & meat products	1	1	1	1	1	1	0	0	1	1	1
Fish & fish dishes	4	10	13	18	13	6	10	16	23	16	14
of which:											
coated &/or fried white fish	3	3	3	4	3	2	2	3	4	3	3
oily fish	1	7	9	13	9	3	7	11	18	11	10
Vegetables (excluding potatoes)	7	8	10	11	10	8	15	12	11	12	11
Potatoes & savoury snacks	26	18	16	14	17	26	18	15	11	16	17
of which:											
chips	22	13	12	10	13	20	13	10	8	11	12
other fried or roast potatoes	2	2	2	3	2	3	2	2	2	2	2
savoury snacks	2	1	1	1	1	2	2	1	1	1	1
Fruit & nuts	1	6	4	3	4	3	2	4	6	4	4
of which:											
nuts & seeds	1	5	3	2	3	2	1	2	4	2	3
Sugar, preserves & confectionery	1	1	1	0	1	1	1	1	1	1	1
Drinks*	0	0	0	0	0	0	0	0	0	0	0
Miscellaneous**	4	6	6	7	6	6	8	9	9	8	7
Average daily intake (g)	**2.10**	**2.30**	**2.31**	**2.29**	**2.27**	**1.69**	**1.60**	**1.68**	**1.82**	**1.71**	**1.98**
Total number of respondents	**108**	**219**	**253**	**253**	**833**	**104**	**210**	**318**	**259**	**891**	**1724**

Note: * Includes soft drinks, alcoholic drinks, tea, coffee and water.
 ** Includes powdered beverages (except tea and coffee), soups, sauces, condiments and artificial sweeteners.

Table 5.19

Percentage contribution of food types to average daily intake of *cis* n–6 polyunsaturated fatty acids by sex and age of respondent

Percentages

Type of food	Men aged (years):				All men	Women aged (years):				All women	All
	19–24	25–34	35–49	50–64		19–24	25–34	35–49	50–64		
	%	%	%	%	%	%	%	%	%	%	%
Cereals & cereal products	20	20	20	20	20	20	20	20	22	20	20
of which:											
pizza	4	2	1	1	2	2	2	1	1	1	2
white bread	4	4	5	4	4	7	4	3	3	4	4
whole grain & high fibre breakfast cereals	1	2	2	2	2	1	1	2	3	2	2
biscuits	1	2	2	2	2	1	2	2	3	2	2
buns, cakes & pastries	2	2	3	4	3	1	3	3	4	3	3
Milk & milk products	2	2	3	3	2	2	3	3	3	3	3
Eggs & egg dishes	4	4	4	5	4	3	3	3	4	3	4
Fat spreads	15	14	14	17	15	8	11	12	14	12	14
of which:											
butter	0	0	0	1	0	0	0	0	1	0	0
margarines	2	2	2	1	2	1	1	2	2	1	1
polyunsaturated reduced fat spreads (60–80% fat)	7	4	7	8	7	1	5	4	6	5	6
other reduced fat spreads (60–80% fat)	3	4	3	3	4	4	2	3	3	3	3
low fat spreads (40% fat or less)	2	3	2	3	2	1	3	2	2	2	2
Meat & meat products	24	20	20	18	20	18	15	16	15	16	18
of which:											
bacon & ham	3	2	2	3	2	1	1	1	2	1	2
beef, veal & dishes	2	2	1	1	1	2	1	1	1	1	1
lamb & dishes	0	1	1	0	1	0	0	1	1	0	0
pork & dishes	1	1	1	1	1	1	1	1	1	1	1
coated chicken & turkey	3	2	2	1	2	4	2	3	1	2	2
chicken, turkey & dishes	5	5	6	4	5	5	5	5	4	5	5
burgers & kebabs	3	2	1	0	1	1	1	1	0	1	1
sausages	4	3	3	2	3	2	2	2	2	2	2
meat pies & pastries	3	3	3	3	3	2	2	2	2	2	2
other meat & meat products	0	1	1	1	1	1	0	0	1	1	1
Fish & fish dishes	3	3	4	5	4	3	4	5	6	5	4
of which:											
coated &/or fried white fish	3	2	3	3	3	2	2	3	4	3	3
Vegetables (excluding potatoes)	4	6	9	9	7	6	13	10	9	10	9
Potatoes & savoury snacks	19	14	13	11	13	20	15	12	10	13	13
of which:											
chips	12	8	7	6	8	11	7	6	6	7	7
other fried or roast potatoes	1	2	1	2	2	1	1	1	1	1	1
savoury snacks	5	4	3	2	3	6	4	3	2	3	3
Fruit & nuts	0	3	3	3	3	4	2	3	4	3	3
of which:											
nuts & seeds	0	3	3	2	2	3	2	2	3	2	2
Sugar, preserves & confectionery	2	2	1	1	1	2	1	2	1	1	1
Drinks*	0	0	0	0	0	0	0	0	0	0	0
Miscellaneous**	8	11	10	9	10	15	13	14	12	13	11
Average daily intake (g)	**12.6**	**13.1**	**13.1**	**12.6**	**12.9**	**10.1**	**9.4**	**9.5**	**8.8**	**9.4**	**11.1**
Total number of respondents	**108**	**219**	**253**	**253**	**833**	**104**	**210**	**318**	**259**	**891**	**1724**

Note: * Includes soft drinks, alcoholic drinks, tea, coffee and water.

** Includes powdered beverages (except tea and coffee), soups, sauces, condiments and artificial sweeteners.

Table 5.20

Average daily intake of total fat and fatty acids (g) and percentage of food energy from total fat and fatty acids by sex of respondent and region

Grams and percentages

Fat and fatty acids	Region											
	Scotland			Northern			Central, South West and Wales			London and the South East		
	Mean	Median	sd	Mean	Median	sd	Mean	Median	sd	Mean	Median	sd
Men												
Total fat (g)	88.1	84.3	28.73	81.7	80.4	25.39	90.1	87.0	28.90	86.4	83.5	29.17
Saturated fatty acids (g)	32.0	30.3	11.86	30.8	29.6	11.36	34.3	33.6	12.55	32.2	31.2	12.25
Trans fatty acids (g)	2.91	2.91	1.333	2.66	2.52	1.181	3.12	2.74	1.538	2.90	2.57	1.567
Cis monounsaturated fatty acids (g)	29.9	28.7	9.36	27.5	26.3	8.90	30.4	29.5	10.07	29.0	28.5	10.10
Cis n-3 polyunsaturated fatty acids (g)	2.48	2.29	1.218	2.10	1.90	0.886	2.29	2.17	0.848	2.37	2.15	1.070
Cis n-6 polyunsaturated fatty acids (g)	14.2	12.1	8.54	12.2	11.7	4.30	13.0	12.7	4.91	13.1	12.6	5.35
Women												
Total fat (g)	59.0	59.7	18.84	58.6	56.1	21.39	61.7	60.5	20.19	64.1	61.9	24.09
Saturated fatty acids (g)	23.0	21.9	7.93	22.4	21.0	9.22	23.3	22.4	9.08	24.2	23.6	10.73
Trans fatty acids (g)	1.89	1.76	0.831	1.99	1.84	0.983	2.12	2.07	0.956	2.03	1.78	1.136
Cis monounsaturated fatty acids (g)	19.1	19.0	6.47	19.0	18.6	7.17	20.4	20.0	7.06	21.1	20.1	8.03
Cis n-3 polyunsaturated fatty acids (g)	1.58	1.46	0.577	1.63	1.49	0.683	1.70	1.60	0.712	1.81	1.62	0.924
Cis n-6 polyunsaturated fatty acids (g)	8.7	8.0	3.95	8.9	8.5	3.88	9.4	9.1	3.81	9.9	9.3	4.19
Percentage food energy from:												
Men												
Total fat	36.0	35.4	4.80	35.1	35.1	5.54	36.1	36.1	5.36	36.0	36.4	6.21
Saturated fatty acids	13.1	12.9	2.40	13.1	13.1	2.88	13.7	13.6	2.93	13.4	13.6	3.10
Trans fatty acids	1.2	1.1	0.44	1.1	1.1	0.38	1.2	1.2	0.44	1.2	1.2	0.46
Cis monounsaturated fatty acids	12.3	12.0	2.05	11.9	11.9	2.32	12.2	12.2	2.12	12.1	12.1	2.51
Cis n-3 polyunsaturated fatty acids	1.0	0.9	0.52	0.9	0.8	0.36	0.9	0.9	0.32	1.0	0.9	0.39
Cis n-6 polyunsaturated fatty acids	5.7	5.3	2.13	5.3	5.1	1.40	5.3	5.0	1.49	5.4	5.2	1.60
Women												
Total fat	34.6	35.1	5.72	33.9	34.1	6.03	34.8	35.1	6.55	35.8	35.7	6.96
Saturated fatty acids	13.5	13.4	2.81	12.9	12.8	2.97	13.1	12.9	3.35	13.4	13.3	3.67
Trans fatty acids	1.1	1.1	0.36	1.1	1.1	0.40	1.2	1.1	0.44	1.1	1.1	0.43
Cis monounsaturated fatty acids	11.2	11.1	2.16	11.0	11.0	2.45	11.5	11.5	2.58	11.8	11.7	2.74
Cis n-3 polyunsaturated fatty acids	0.9	0.9	0.25	1.0	0.9	0.44	1.0	0.9	0.35	1.0	0.9	0.58
Cis n-6 polyunsaturated fatty acids	5.1	4.8	1.65	5.2	4.9	1.57	5.3	5.2	1.60	5.5	5.4	1.72
Total number of men		65			234			294			240	
Total number of women		66			229			327			268	

Table 5.21

Average daily intake of total fat and fatty acids (g) and percentage of food energy from total fat and fatty acids by sex of respondent and whether someone in respondent's household was receiving certain benefits

Grams and percentages

| Fat and fatty acids | Whether receiving benefits | | | | | |
| | Receiving benefits | | | Not receiving benefits | | |
	Mean	Median	sd	Mean	Median	sd
Men						
Total fat (g)	81.5	78.7	29.60	87.2	84.7	27.89
Saturated fatty acids (g)	30.6	29.0	12.41	32.8	31.4	12.08
Trans fatty acids (g)	2.81	2.50	1.400	2.92	2.63	1.460
Cis monounsaturated fatty acids (g)	27.8	25.7	10.79	29.3	28.5	9.59
Cis n-3 polyunsaturated fatty acids (g)	2.13	1.97	0.930	2.30	2.13	0.970
Cis n-6 polyunsaturated fatty acids (g)	14.2	12.1	8.54	12.2	11.7	4.30
Women						
Total fat (g)	56.4	54.0	23.63	62.5	61.0	21.19
Saturated fatty acids (g)	21.4	20.4	9.75	23.7	22.5	9.50
Trans fatty acids (g)	1.86	1.67	1.009	2.08	1.94	1.010
Cis monounsaturated fatty acids (g)	18.7	17.6	8.26	20.5	20.0	7.17
Cis n-3 polyunsaturated fatty acids (g)	1.50	1.38	0.790	1.75	1.60	0.760
Cis n-6 polyunsaturated fatty acids (g)	8.5	7.7	4.43	9.6	9.1	3.85
Percentage food energy from:						
Men						
Total fat	35.8	35.5	5.83	35.8	36.0	5.61
Saturated fatty acids	13.3	13.1	3.16	13.4	13.4	2.90
Trans fatty acids	1.2	1.2	0.42	1.2	1.2	0.43
Cis monounsaturated fatty acids	12.2	12.5	2.44	12.1	12.0	2.27
Cis n-3 polyunsaturated fatty acids	1.0	0.9	0.40	1.0	0.9	0.37
Cis n-6 polyunsaturated fatty acids	5.2	4.9	1.70	5.4	5.2	1.54
Women						
Total fat	34.4	34.8	6.19	35.0	35.0	6.59
Saturated fatty acids	13.0	13.2	2.83	13.2	13.1	3.42
Trans fatty acids	1.1	1.1	0.43	1.2	1.1	0.42
Cis monounsaturated fatty acids	11.4	11.5	2.66	11.5	11.4	2.57
Cis n-3 polyunsaturated fatty acids	1.0	0.9	0.62	1.0	0.9	0.40
Cis n-6 polyunsaturated fatty acids	5.2	4.8	1.70	5.4	5.2	1.62
Total number of men		*110*			*723*	
Total number of women		*150*			*741*	

6 Comparison with other surveys

6.1 Introduction

This chapter compares data from this survey on intakes of energy and macronutrients with comparable data from other surveys, including the Dietary and Nutritional Survey of British Adults aged 16 to 64 years carried out in 1986/87 (1986/87 Adults Survey)[1].

Table 6.1 shows total energy intake, and the percentage of total energy derived from protein, carbohydrates and alcohol, and the percentage of total and food energy derived from fat and fatty acids for the 1986/87 Adults Survey and the current survey[2]. Data are presented for men and women by age. Comparisons are made between comparable age groups in the two surveys; no attempt is made to use the data to undertake cohort analysis. It should be noted that in the 1986/87 Adults Survey the youngest age group was adults aged 16 to 24 years, while in the current NDNS the youngest age group is adults aged 19 to 24 years. This should be borne in mind where there are differences between these groups. A summary of the methodology and findings from the 1986/87 Adults Survey is given in Appendix S of the Technical Report[3].

6.2 Comparison of macronutrient intakes between 1986/87 Adults Survey and present NDNS

Comparisons between the 1986/87 and 2000/01 data show that, overall, men in the current survey had a significantly lower mean daily energy intake than those in 1986/87, 9.72MJ and 10.30MJ respectively (p<0.01). There were no significant differences in mean daily energy intake between the two surveys for women.

Overall, the data show that men and women in the current survey derived a significantly higher proportion of their energy from protein and carbohydrate and a significantly lower proportion from fat than in 1986/87. These changes are in line with trends seen in the National Food Survey[4].

For example, men in 2000/01 derived 44.7% of their total energy from carbohydrate and 15.4% from protein compared with 41.6% and 14.1%, respectively, in the earlier survey (p<0.01). This difference was significant for men of all ages and women aged 25 to 64 years for energy from carbohydrates and for men aged 25 to 64 years for energy derived from protein.

Overall, men and women in the current survey derived a significantly lower proportion of their energy from total fat and saturated, *trans* and *cis* monounsaturated fatty acids and a significantly higher proportion from *cis* n-3 polyunsaturated fatty acids than those in the 1986/87 Adults Survey. For example, men and women in 2000/01 derived 33.5% of their total energy from total fat compared with 37.6% for men and 39.2% for women in the earlier survey (p<0.01). These differences were significant for all sex and age groups for energy from total fat and saturated and *trans* fatty acids. For men, there were no significant differences in the proportion of energy derived from *cis* monounsaturated fatty acids between the two surveys for the different age groups. However, for women, those aged 25 to 64 years in the current survey derived a significantly lower proportion of their energy from this source than those in the earlier survey (25 to 34: p<0.05: all others: p<0.01).

The proportion of energy derived from *cis* n-3 polyunsaturated fatty acids was significantly higher for men aged 25 to 64 years and women of all age groups in this survey than in the earlier survey. For example, the oldest group of men and women in 2000/01 derived, respectively, 0.9% and 1.0% of their energy from *cis* n-3 polyunsaturated fatty acids compared with 0.7% for those aged 50 to 64 years in 1986/87 (p<0.01).

The percentage of energy derived from alcohol for respondents, including non-consumers, was significantly higher for women overall, and for the youngest and the oldest group of women in the current survey than in the earlier survey (16/19 to 24: p<0.05; all others: p<0.01). There were no significant differences in the percentage of energy derived from alcohol between the two surveys for men overall or by age.

In this survey, the percentage of total and food energy derived from carbohydrate is lower, and the percentage from total fat and saturated fatty acids higher, than the appropriate DRV for sex and age groups[5]. However, intakes as a percentage of energy are closer to the appropriate DRV than they were in the 1986/87 Adults Survey. For example, the DRV for carbohydrate as a percentage of daily total energy intake for men aged 19 to 50 years is 47%. In the current survey, men aged 25 to 34 years derived 44.6% of their daily total energy intake from carbohydrate compared with 40.9% for men of this age in 1986/87. The DRVs for fat and saturated fatty acids as a percentage of daily total energy intake for men aged 19 to 50 years are 33% and 10% respectively. In the current survey, men aged 25 to 34 years derived 33.5% of their total daily energy intake from total fat and 12.3% from saturated fatty acids, compared with 37.9% and 15.3% respectively for men of this age in 1986/87.

(Table 6.1)

6.3 Comparisons with other non-government surveys

Table 6.2 shows data from two other published studies on energy intakes and the contribution of macronutrients to energy intake: the 1993/97 European Prospective Investigation of Cancer (EPIC) in Norfolk[6], and the 1997/99 North/South Ireland Food Consumption Survey[7]. It should be noted that these have focussed on special population sub-groups or geographic areas and may not be representative of the population of adults aged 19 to 64 years in Great Britain. Further, while both studies used a seven-day dietary diary as the method of collecting information on dietary intake, neither the EPIC-Norfolk study nor the North/South Ireland Food Consumption Survey had the respondent weigh the food and drinks consumed[8]. These factors need to be taken into account when comparing with data from the 2000/01 NDNS.

The data from these two studies confirm the findings from this survey in that intake of energy is below the Estimated Average Requirement for women in both studies, and for men in the EPIC-Norfolk study[9]. Data from the EPIC-Norfolk study and the North/South Ireland Food Consumption Survey show similar percentage contributions to energy intake from protein, carbohydrate and fat to the 2000/01 NDNS. The North/South Ireland Food Consumption Survey also confirms the finding in the 2000/01 NDNS that the percentage of energy derived from carbohydrates is lower, and the percentage of energy derived from fat is higher, than the DRV[5].

(Table 6.2)

References and endnotes

[1] Gregory J, Foster K, Tyler H, Wiseman M. *The Dietary and Nutritional Survey of British Adults*. HMSO (London, 1990).

[2] Comparisons are made on the basis of total energy because intakes of protein and carbohydrate as a percentage of food energy were not available in the 1986/87 Adults Survey.

[3] The Technical Report is available online at http://www.food.gov.uk/science.

[4] Department for Environment, Food & Rural Affairs. *National Food Survey 2000*. TSO (London, 2001).

[5] The Dietary Reference Values (DRVs) for carbohydrate, fat and saturated fatty acids for adults as a percentage of total energy intake (percentage of food energy) are:

Total carbohydrate: 47 (50)

Total fat: 33 (35)

Saturated fatty acids: 10 (11)

Source: Department of Health. Report on Health and Social Subjects: 41. *Dietary Reference Values for Food Energy and Nutrients for the United Kingdom*. HMSO (London, 1991).

[6] Bingham SA, Welch AA, McTaggart A, Mulligan AA, Runswick SA, Luben R, Oakes S, Khaw KT, Wareham N, Day NE. Nutritional methods in the European Prospective Investigation of Cancer in Norfolk. *Public Health Nutrition* 2001; **4**(3): 847-858.

[7] Harrington KE, McGowan MJ, Kiely M, Robson PJ, Livingstone MBE, Morrissey PA, Gibney MJ. Macronutrient intakes and food sources in Irish adults: findings of the North/South Ireland Food Consumption Survey. *Public Health Nutrition* 2001; **4**(5A): 1051-1060.

[8] The EPIC study and the North/South Ireland Study both used a seven-day dietary diary, but the respondent did not weigh any of the food or drinks consumed. Quantification of amounts eaten was calculated using a variety of methods.

[9] The Estimated Average Requirements (EARs) for energy are:

Men aged 19 to 50: 10.60MJ/d	Women aged 19 to 50: 8.10MJ/d
Men aged 51 to 59: 10.60MJ/d	Women aged 51 to 59: 8.00MJ/d
Men aged 60 to 64: 9.93MJ/d	Women aged 60 to 64: 7.99MJ/d

Source: Department of Health. Report on Health and Social Subjects: 41. *Dietary Reference Values for Food Energy and Nutrients for the United Kingdom*. HMSO (London, 1991).

Table 6.1

Comparison of average daily energy intakes and percentage contribution to energy intakes from macronutrients with the 1986/87 Adults Survey

MJs and percentages

Macronutrients	Age of respondent (years):									
	1986/87 Adults Survey*				All	2000/01 NDNS				All
	16–24	25–34	35–49	50–64		19–24	25–34	35–49	50–64	
Men										
Energy (MJ)										
mean daily total energy intake	10.29	10.21	10.46	9.96	10.30	9.44	9.82	9.93	9.55	9.72
Total carbohydrate										
% food energy from carbohydrate**	..	..	..	..	44.7	49.0	47.7	47.5	47.4	47.7
% total energy from carbohydrate	42.9	40.9	41.5	41.4	41.6	46.0	44.6	44.4	44.6	44.7
Protein										
% food energy from protein**	..	..	..	..	15.2	14.9	16.5	16.7	17.0	16.5
% total energy from protein	13.7	14.1	13.9	14.7	14.1	14.0	15.4	15.5	15.9	15.4
Alcohol***										
% total energy from alcohol	5.9	7.3	7.6	6.4	6.9	6.0	6.6	6.8	6.4	6.5
Total fat										
% food energy from total fat	40.2	41.0	40.2	40.2	40.4	36.0	35.8	35.9	35.6	35.8
% total energy from total fat	37.9	37.9	37.1	37.6	37.6	34.0	33.5	33.4	33.3	33.5
Saturated fatty acids										
% food energy from saturated fatty acids	16.1	16.5	16.3	17.2	16.5	13.5	13.2	13.5	13.4	13.4
% total energy from saturated fatty acids	15.2	15.3	15.1	16.1	15.4	12.8	12.3	12.6	12.6	12.6
Trans fatty acids										
% food energy from *trans* fatty acids	2.3	2.2	2.2	2.1	2.2	1.2	1.2	1.2	1.2	1.2
% total energy from *trans* fatty acids	2.1	2.0	2.1	2.0	2.0	1.2	1.1	1.1	1.1	1.1
Cis monounsaturated fatty acids										
% food energy from *cis* monounsaturated fatty acids	12.6	12.8	12.3	12.1	12.4	12.4	12.3	12.0	11.8	12.1
% total energy from *cis* monounsaturated fatty acids	11.9	11.8	11.3	11.3	11.6	11.7	11.5	11.2	11.0	11.3
Cis n–3 polyunsaturated fatty acids										
% food energy from *cis* n–3 polyunsaturated fatty acids	0.8	0.8	0.8	0.7	0.8	0.9	1.0	1.0	1.0	1.0
% total energy from *cis* n–3 polyunsaturated fatty acids	0.7	0.8	0.7	0.7	0.7	0.9	0.9	0.9	0.9	0.9
Cis n–6 polyunsaturated fatty acids										
% food energy from *cis* n–6 polyunsaturated fatty acids	5.5	5.7	5.6	4.9	5.4	5.3	5.4	5.4	5.3	5.4
% total energy from *cis* n–6 polyunsaturated fatty acids	5.2	5.3	5.2	4.6	5.1	5.0	5.1	5.0	4.9	5.0
Base – number of men	214	254	346	273	1087	108	219	253	253	833
Women										
Energy (MJ)										
mean daily total energy intake	7.11	6.99	7.24	6.74	7.05	7.00	6.61	6.96	6.91	6.87
Total carbohydrate										
% food energy from carbohydrate**	..	..	..	..	44.2	49.1	48.7	48.6	48.1	48.5
% total energy from carbohydrate	44.9	43.0	42.5	42.3	43.0	47.0	46.8	46.8	46.4	46.7
Protein										
% food energy from protein**	..	..	..	..	15.6	15.4	15.9	16.7	17.4	16.6
% total energy from protein	14.0	14.6	15.4	16.1	15.2	14.8	15.3	16.1	16.8	15.9
Alcohol***										
% total energy from alcohol	2.5	3.1	3.2	2.2	2.8	4.6	4.0	3.9	3.7	3.9
Total fat										
% food energy from total fat	39.8	40.7	40.3	40.3	40.3	35.5	35.4	34.7	34.5	34.9
% total energy from total fat	38.7	39.4	39.0	39.5	39.2	33.8	34.0	33.3	33.3	33.5
Saturated fatty acids										
% food energy from saturated fatty acids	16.4	16.9	16.9	17.5	17.0	12.9	13.2	13.2	13.3	13.2
% total energy from saturated fatty acids	16.0	16.4	16.4	17.1	16.5	12.8	12.3	12.6	12.6	12.6
Trans fatty acids										
% food energy from *trans* fatty acids	2.2	2.2	2.2	2.1	2.2	1.1	1.1	1.2	1.2	1.2
% total energy from *trans* fatty acids	2.1	2.1	2.1	2.1	2.1	1.1	1.1	1.1	1.1	1.1
Cis monounsaturated fatty acids										
% food energy from *cis* monounsaturated fatty acids	12.3	12.4	12.2	12.0	12.2	12.2	11.7	11.3	11.1	11.5
% total energy from *cis* monounsaturated fatty acids	12.0	12.0	11.8	11.7	11.8	11.6	11.3	10.9	10.7	11.0
Cis n–3 polyunsaturated fatty acids										
% food energy from *cis* n–3 polyunsaturated fatty acids	0.8	0.8	0.7	0.7	0.8	1.0	1.0	1.0	1.1	1.0
% total energy from *cis* n–3 polyusaturated fatty acids	0.8	0.7	0.7	0.7	0.7	0.9	0.9	0.9	1.0	1.0
Cis n–6 polyunsaturated fatty acids										
% food energy from *cis* n–6 polyunsaturated fatty acids	5.3	5.5	5.3	5.0	5.3	5.6	5.6	5.3	5.0	5.3
% total energy from *cis* n–6 polyusaturated fatty acids	5.2	5.3	5.2	4.9	5.1	5.4	5.4	5.1	4.8	5.1
Base – number of women	189	253	385	283	1110	104	210	318	259	891

Note: * 1986/87 Gregory JR et al. The Dietary and Nutritional Survey of British Adults. HMSO (London, 1990).

** Data on the percentage of food energy derived from carbohydrate and protein are not available for the 1986/87 Adults Survey .

*** Data on the percentage of total energy derived from alcohol is based on the total sample, that is including non–consumers.

Table 6.2

Comparison of average daily energy intakes and percentage contribution to energy intakes from macronutrients with other surveys of adults

MJs and percentages

Reference (study date)	Age (years)	Sex	Sample size	Energy (MJ) intake/day	Percentage of food energy from:			Percentage of total energy from:			
					carbo-hydrate*	protein*	total fat*	carbo-hydrate	protein	alcohol	total fat
Dietary and Nutritional Survey	16 to 64	M	1087	10.30	44.7	15.2	40.4	41.6	14.1	6.9	37.6
of British Adults (1986/87)**		F	1110	7.05	44.2	15.6	40.3	43.0	15.2	2.8	39.2
Bingham (1993/97)***	45 to 54	M	140	9.91	..	..	..	46.0	15.0	4.0	33.0
		F	334	7.31	..	..	..	47.0	16.0	4.0	33.0
	55 to 64	M	328	9.29	..	..	..	47.0	15.0	5.0	33.0
		F	423	6.89	..	..	..	47.0	16.0	3.0	33.0
North/South Ireland Food	18 to 64	M	662	11.0	46.2	16.6	37.0	43.5	15.5	5.9	34.8
Consumption Survey (1997/99)****		F	717	7.6	46.6	16.2	36.9	45.1	15.6	3.5	35.6
National Diet and Nutrition	19 to 64	M	833	9.72	47.7	16.5	35.8	44.7	15.4	6.5	33.5
Survey (2000/01)		F	891	6.87	48.5	16.6	34.9	46.7	15.9	3.9	33.5

Note: * Data on the percentage of food energy from carbohydrate, protein and total fat were not available for Bingham et al (1993/97).

** Gregory JR et al. The Dietary and Nutritional Survey of British Adults. HMSO (London, 1990).

*** Bingham SA, Welch A, McTaggart A, Mulligan A et al. Nutritional methods in the European Prospective Investigation of Cancer in Norfolk. Public Health Nutrition 2001; 4(3): 847–858.

**** Harrington KE, McGowan MJ, Kiley M, Robson PJ, Livingstone MBE, Morrissey PA and Gibney MJ. Macronutrient intakes and food sources in Irish adults: findings of the North/South Food Consumption Survey. Public Health Nutrition 2001; 4(5A): 1051–1060.

Appendix A   Sampling errors and statistical methods

1   Sampling errors

This section examines the sources of error associated with survey estimates and presents sampling errors of survey estimates, referred to as standard errors, and design factors for a number of key variables shown in this volume. It should be noted that tables showing standard errors in the main part of this volume have assumed a simple random sample design. In testing for the significance of the differences between two survey estimates, proportions or means, the standard error calculated as for a simple random sample design was multiplied by an assumed, conservative, design factor of 1.5 to allow for the complex sample design.

The estimates presented in the main part of this volume are based on data weighted to correct for differential sampling probability and for differential non-response. The sampling errors presented in this appendix were calculated after applying a weight to compensate for differential sampling probability and differential non-response. The sample was also post-stratified, so that it matched the population distribution in terms of age, sex and region[1].

1.1   The accuracy of survey results

Survey results are subject to various sources of error. The total error in a survey estimate is the difference between the estimate derived from the data collected and the true value for the population. It can be thought of as being comprised of random and systematic errors, and each of these two main types of error can be subdivided into error from a number of different sources.

1.1.1 Random error

Random error is the part of the total error which would be expected to average zero if a number of repeats of the same survey were carried out based on different samples from the same population.

An important component of random error is sampling error, which arises because the estimate is based on a survey rather than a census of the population. The results of this or any other survey would be expected to vary from the true population values. The amount of variation depends on both the size of the sample and the sample design.

Random error may also arise from other sources such as the respondent's interpretation of the questions. As with all surveys carried out by the Social Survey Division (SSD), considerable efforts were made on this survey to minimise these effects through interviewer training and through feasibility work; however, it is likely some will remain that are not possible to quantify.

1.1.2 Systematic error

Systematic error, or bias, applies to those sources of error that will not average to zero over a number of repeats of the survey. The category includes, for example, bias due to omission of certain parts of the population from the sampling frame, or bias due to interviewer or coder variation. A substantial effort is put into avoiding systematic errors but it is likely that some will remain.

Non-response bias is a systematic error that is of particular concern. It occurs if non-respondents to the survey, or to particular elements of the survey, differ significantly in some respect from respondents, so that the responding sample is not representative of the total population. Non-response can be minimised by training interviewers in how to deal with potential refusals and in strategies to minimise non-contacts. However, a certain level of non-response is inevitable in any voluntary survey. The resulting bias is, however, dependent not only on the absolute level of non-response, but on the extent to which non-respondents differ from respondents in terms of the measures that the survey aims to estimate.

Although respondents were encouraged to take part in all components of the survey, some refused certain components. Chapter 2 of the Technical Report[2] examines the characteristics of groups responding to the different parts of the survey package. The analysis of the region, sex and age profile of respondents compared with population estimates showed evidence of some response bias. In particular, there was an under representation of men and of people aged 19 to 24 years. The data for the main part of this volume (and all volumes in the series) were therefore weighted for differential non-response by sex, age and region.

1.2   Standard errors for estimates for the NDNS of adults aged 19 to 64 years

As described in Chapter 1 and Appendix D of the Technical Report[2], this survey used a complex sample design, which involved both clustering and stratification. In considering the accuracy of estimates, standard errors calculated on the basis of a simple random sample design will be incorrect because of the complex sample design.

This dietary survey sample was clustered using postcode sectors as primary sampling units (PSUs). Clustering can increase standard errors if there is a lot of variation in characteristics between the PSUs, but little variation within them. By contrast, stratification tends to reduce standard errors especially where the stratification factors are correlated to the survey estimate. Stratifiying the sample ensures that certain sections of the population are represented in the sample. The main stratifier used on this survey was Standard Statistical Region (SSR). The PSUs were further stratified by population density, socio-economic group and car ownership (see Appendix D of the Technical Report[2]).

In a complex sample design, the size of the standard error of any estimate depends on how the characteristic of interest is spread within and between PSUs and strata: this is taken into account by pairing up adjacent PSUs from the same strata. The squared differences in the estimates between successive PSUs from the same strata are calculated and summed to produce the standard error.

The majority of estimates in this survey take the form of ratio estimates, either means or proportions. The formula to calculate the standard error of these is:

$$se\ (r) = \frac{1}{x}\ [var(y) + r^2\ var\ (x) - 2r\ cov(y,x)]^{1/2}$$

where the ratio $r = y/x$.

The method explicitly allows for the fact that the percentages and means are actually ratios of two survey estimates, both of which are subject to random error. The value se (r) is the estimate of the standard error of the ratio, r, expressed in terms of se(y) and se(x) which are the estimated standard errors of y and x, and cov(y, x) which is their estimated covariance. The resulting estimate is slightly biased and only valid if the denominator is not too variable[3]. The ratio means for age groups have standard errors equal to zero for the full sample because both the numerator and the denominator have been set to equal the population totals and thus cannot vary for any selected sample.

The method of standard error estimation compares the successive differences between totals of the characteristic of interest for adjacent PSUs (postal sectors)[4]. The characteristic is the numerator (for example the average daily intake of protein), and the sample size is the denominator in the ratio estimate[5]. The ordering of PSUs reflects the ranking of postal sectors on the stratifiers used in the sample design.

Tables A1 and A2(a) and (b) give standard errors, taking account of the complex sample design used on this survey, for the key variables presented in this volume. Standard errors for estimates of socio-demographic subgroups, such as household benefit status and region, are shown separately for men and women to reflect the way they are presented in the main part of the report. Standard errors are presented for the diary sample only.

1.3   Estimating standard errors for other survey estimates

Although standard errors can be calculated readily by computer, there are practical problems in presenting a large number of survey estimates. One solution is to calculate standard errors for selected variables and, from these, identify design factors appropriate for the specific survey design and for different types of survey variable. The standard error of other survey measures can then be estimated using an appropriate design factor, together with the sampling error assuming a simple random sample.

1.3.1 The Design Factor (*deft*)

The effect of a complex sample design can be quantified by comparing the observed variability in the sample with the expected variability had the survey used a simple random sample. The most commonly used statistic is the design factor (*deft*), which is calculated as a ratio of the standard error for a survey estimate allowing for the full complexity of the sample design (including weighting), to the standard error assuming that the result has come from a simple random sample. The *deft* can be used as a multiplier to the standard error based on a simple random sample, $se(p)_{srs}$, to give the standard error of the complex design, se(p), by using the following formula:

$$se(p)=deft \times se(p)_{srs}$$

Tables A1 and A2(a) and (b) show *deft* values for certain measures for those who completed a seven-day dietary record. The level of *deft* varies between survey variables, reflecting the degree to which the characteristic is clustered within PSUs or is distributed between strata. Variables which are highly correlated to the post-strata should also have reduced *deft* values. For a single variable, the level of the *deft* can also vary according to the size of the subgroup on which the estimate is based because smaller subgroups can be less affected by clustering.

Table A1 shows the *deft* values for a range of socio-demographic variables for the diary sample, and Tables A2(a) and A2(b) for a range of macronutrients. For the socio-demographic variables, where geographic clustering would be expected, six out of ten of the design factors for men and eight out of ten for women are less than 1.2. Design factors of this order are considered to be small and they indicate that, in this survey, the characteristic is not markedly clustered geographically. For two of the ten socio-demographic variables *deft* values are above 1.5 for both sexes.

For men, around 70% of the design factors presented in Table A2(a) are less than 1.2, while for women 74% of those in Table A2(b) are less than 1.2. For both men and women none of the *deft* values are greater than 1.5.

(Tables A1, A2(a) and A2(b))

1.3.2 Testing differences between means and proportions

Standard errors can be used to test whether an observed difference between two proportions or means in the sample is likely to be entirely due to sampling error. An estimate for the standard error of a difference between percentages assuming a simple random sample is:

$$se_1(p_1-p_2) = \surd\,[(p_1 q_1 /n_1) + (p_2 q_2 /n_2)]$$

where p_1 and p_2 are the observed percentages for the two subsamples, q_1 and q_2 are respectively *(100-p_1)* and *(100-p_2)*, and n_1 and n_2 are the subsample sizes.

The equivalent formula for the standard error of the difference between the means for subsamples 1 and 2 is:

$$se_2\,(diff) = \surd\,(se_1{}^2+se_2{}^2)$$

Allowance for the complex sample design is then made by multiplying the standard errors se_1 and se_2 from the above formula by the appropriate *deft* values.

In this volume the calculation of the difference between proportions and means assumed a *deft* value of 1.5 across all survey estimates. The calculation of complex sampling errors and design factors for key characteristics show that this was a conservative estimate for some characteristics for some age and sex groups, but was an optimistic estimate for other characteristics. Therefore there will be some differences in sample proportions and means that are not commented on in the text, but that are significantly different, at least at the p<0.05 level. Equally, there will be some differences that are described as significant in the text, but that are not significantly different when the complex sampling design is taken into account. An indication of the characteristics for which significance tests are likely to provide false-positives or false-negatives can be gained by looking at the size of the *deft* values in the tables in this appendix.

Confidence intervals can be calculated around a survey estimate using the standard error for that estimate. For example, the 95% confidence interval is calculated as 1.96 times the standard error on either side of the estimated proportion or mean value. At the 95% confidence level, over many repeats of the survey under the same conditions, 95% of these confidence intervals would contain the population estimate. However, when assessing the results of a survey, it is usual to assume that there is only a 5% chance that the true population value will fall outside the 95% confidence interval calculated for the survey estimate.

References and endnotes

[1] Weighting for different sampling probabilities results in larger sampling errors than for an equal-probability sample without weights. However, using population totals to control for differential non-response tends to lead to a reduction in the errors. The method used to calculate the sampling errors identifies the weighting for unequal sampling probabilities and to the population separately, and adjusts the sampling errors accordingly.

[2] The Technical Report, including its Appendices, is available online at http://www.food.gov.uk/science.

[3] This variability of the denominator can be measured by the coefficient of variation of x, denoted by $cv(x)$, which is the standard error of x expressed as a proportion of x

$$cv(x) = \frac{se(x)}{x}$$

It has been suggested that the ratio estimator should not be used if $cv(x)$ is greater than 0.2. For the standard errors produced here, the denominators for the ratios were 'number of men' and 'number of women'. Both of these totals were constant, determined by the post-stratification and, therefore, there is no variation in these denominators and hence the cv of the denominator will be zero.

[4] The calculation of standard errors and design factors for this survey used the software package Stata. For further details of the method of calculation see: Elliot D A comparison of software for producing sampling errors on social surveys. *Survey Methodology Bulletin* 1999; **44**: 27–36.

[5] For a survey of this kind the sample size is subject to random fluctuation, both within each PSU and overall. This is because the number of adults identified in each PSU is dependent on which households are sampled and there will be differing amounts of non-response. There is more control in the (weighted) sample sizes of subgroups such as age and sex since these variables were used as post-stratifiers.

Table A1

True standard errors and design factors for socio-demographic characteristics of the diary sample by sex of respondent

Diary sample   Numbers

	Men			Women		
	% (p)	Standard error of p*	Design factor	% (p)	Standard error of p*	Design factor
Age group						
19–24 years	13	0.00	0.00	12	0.00	0.00
25–34 years	26	0.00	0.00	24	0.00	0.00
35–49 years	30	0.00	0.00	36	0.00	0.00
50–64 years	30	0.00	0.00	29	0.00	0.00
Region						
Scotland	8	0.92	0.98	7	0.86	0.98
Northern	28	1.14	0.73	26	0.96	0.65
Central, South West and						
Wales	35	2.54	1.54	37	2.62	1.62
London and the South East	29	2.48	1.58	30	2.57	1.67
Household receipt of benefits						
Receiving benefits	13	1.47	1.25	17	1.47	1.17
Not receiving benefits	87	1.47	1.25	83	1.47	1.17
Sample size		*833*			*891*	

Note: * The ratio means for age groups for the diary sample have standard errors equal to zero because both the numerator and the denominator have been set to equal the population totals and thus cannot vary for any selected sample.

Table A2(a)

True standard errors and design factors for average daily intakes of energy and macronutrients by age of respondent: men

Diary sample

Macronutrients	Men aged (years):								
	19-24			25-34			35-49		
	Mean r	Standard error of r	Design factor	Mean r	Standard error of r	Design factor	Mean r	Standard error of r	Design factor
Energy (kcal)	2247	65	1.30	2337	44	1.11	2361	39	1.01
Energy (MJ)	9.44	0.27	1.30	9.82	0.18	1.11	9.23	0.16	1.01
Protein (g)	77.8	2.28	1.27	90.6	3.82	1.11	90.1	1.51	1.03
% food energy from protein	14.9	0.33	1.31	16.5	0.40	1.26	16.7	0.18	0.97
Total carbohydrate (g)	273	8.0	1.34	277	6.0	1.18	279	5.6	1.03
% food energy from carbohydrate	49	0.8	1.35	48	0.5	1.28	47	0.4	0.94
Alcohol (g)	20.4	3.16	1.30	22.2	1.56	0.96	23.1	1.40	0.94
% energy from alcohol	6.0	0.96	1.34	6.6	0.47	1.00	6.8	0.42	0.97
Total fat (g)	85.8	3.72	1.33	87.1	2.27	1.20	88.3	1.75	0.96
Saturated fatty acids (g)	32.3	1.62	1.39	32.2	0.95	1.19	33.4	0.77	0.98
Trans fatty acids (g)	2.95	0.16	1.34	2.86	0.11	1.13	2.98	0.09	0.91
Cis monounsaturated fatty acids (g)	29.6	1.31	1.30	29.9	0.80	1.25	29.6	0.57	0.90
Cis n-3 polyunsaturated fatty acids (g)	2.10	0.09	1.30	2.30	0.10	1.38	2.31	0.05	0.83
Cis n-6 polyunsaturated fatty acids (g)	12.6	0.68	1.32	13.1	0.36	1.17	13.1	0.31	0.99
Cholesterol (mg)	269	17.0	1.33	298	11.0	1.36	309	9.0	1.11
% food energy from total fat	36.0	0.78	1.35	35.8	0.43	1.17	35.9	0.32	0.90
Sample size	108			219			253		

Table A2(b)

True standard errors and design factors for average daily intakes of energy and macronutrients by age of respondent: women

Diary sample

Macronutrients	Women aged (years):								
	19-24			25-34			35-49		
	Mean r	Standard error of r	Design factor	Mean r	Standard error of r	Design factor	Mean r	Standard error of r	Design factor
Energy (kcal)	1665	60	1.35	1570	27	1.00	1654	24	1.03
Energy (MJ)	7.00	0.25	1.35	6.61	0.11	1.00	6.96	0.10	1.02
Protein (g)	59.9	2.06	1.29	58.7	1.14	1.06	65.1	1.03	1.09
% food energy from protein	15.5	0.47	1.35	15.9	0.31	1.26	16.7	0.19	0.97
Total carbohydrate (g)	206	7.9	1.31	196	3.8	1.05	206	3.5	1.02
% food energy from total carbohydrate	49	1.0	1.25	49	0.4	1.07	49	0.4	1.13
Alcohol (g)	11.4	1.73	1.22	9.1	0.89	1.14	9.2	0.61	0.89
% energy from alcohol	4.6	0.64	1.19	4.0	0.37	1.12	3.9	0.27	0.92
Total fat (g)	63.9	3.53	1.37	29.8	1.30	0.95	61.9	1.14	0.95
Saturated fatty acids (g)	23.5	1.58	1.36	22.4	0.59	1.04	23.6	0.54	1.05
Trans fatty acids (g)	2.00	0.13	1.17	1.93	0.06	1.04	2.06	0.04	0.77
Cis monounsaturated fatty acids (g)	21.8	1.14	1.34	19.9	0.44	0.93	20.2	0.39	0.96
Cis n-3 polyunsaturated fatty acids (g)	1.69	0.09	1.22	1.60	0.05	1.12	1.68	0.05	1.12
Cis n-6 polyunsaturated fatty acids (g)	10.1	0.63	1.31	9.4	0.24	0.88	9.5	0.18	0.85
Cholesterol (mg)	196	14.3	1.31	188	5.6	0.98	214	5.4	1.04
% food energy from total fat	35.5	0.90	1.22	35.4	0.44	1.08	34.7	0.36	1.01
Sample size	104			210			318		

Numbers

	All men					
50-64						
Mean r	Standard error of r	Design factor	Mean r	Standard error of r	Design factor	
2271	42	1.17	2312	21	1.03	Energy (kcal)
9.55	0.17	1.17	9.72	0.09	1.03	Energy (MJ)
88.8	1.50	1.04	88.2	1.12	0.99	Protein (g)
17.0	0.20	0.94	16.5	0.14	1.09	% food energy from protein
269	5.3	1.06	275	3.0	1.08	Total carbohydrate (g)
47	0.4	1.13	48	0.2	1.04	% food energy from total carbohydrate
21.1	1.88	1.16	21.93	0.95	1.11	Alcohol (g)
6.4	0.55	1.16	6.5	0.28	1.14	% energy from alcohol
84.5	2.03	1.20	86.5	1.06	1.09	Total fat (g)
32.0	0.90	1.21	32.5	0.45	1.08	Saturated fatty acids (g)
2.86	0.10	1.11	2.91	0.05	1.01	*Trans* fatty acids (g)
27.9	0.66	1.14	29.1	0.36	1.07	*Cis* monounsaturated fatty acids (g)
2.29	0.07	1.20	2.27	0.03	1.02	*Cis* n-3 polyunsaturated fatty acids (g)
12.6	0.48	1.24	12.9	0.22	1.23	*Cis* n-6 polyunsaturated fatty acids (g)
319	7.8	0.97	304	4.5	1.01	Cholesterol (mg)
35.6	0.44	1.22	35.8	0.22	1.11	% food energy from total fat
	253			833		*Sample size*

Numbers

	All women					
50-64						
Mean r	Standard error of r	Design factor	Mean r	Standard error of r	Design factor	
1642	31	1.20	1632	17	1.21	Energy (kcal)
6.91	0.13	1.20	6.87	0.07	1.21	Energy (MJ)
67.4	1.06	1.08	63.7	0.73	1.30	Protein (g)
17.4	0.19	0.94	16.6	0.14	1.15	% food energy from protein
203	4.2	1.12	203	2.3	1.16	Total carbohydrate (g)
48	0.4	0.93	48	0.3	1.15	% food energy from total carbohydrate
8.6	0.73	1.03	9.3	0.43	1.06	Alcohol (g)
3.7	0.32	1.04	3.9	0.18	1.07	% energy from alcohol
61.2	1.58	1.18	61.4	0.83	1.14	Total fat (g)
23.7	0.68	1.12	23.3	0.37	1.15	Saturated fatty acids (g)
2.12	0.07	1.07	2.04	0.04	1.12	*Trans* fatty acids (g)
19.7	0.52	1.16	20.2	0.29	1.18	*Cis* monounsaturated fatty acids (g)
1.82	0.05	0.97	1.71	0.03	1.16	*Cis* n-3 polyunsaturated fatty acids (g)
8.8	0.28	1.29	9.4	0.13	0.95	*Cis* n-6 polyunsaturated fatty acids (g)
239	6.6	1.14	213	4.1	1.3	Cholesterol (mg)
34.5	0.44	1.05	34.9	0.24	1.08	% food energy from total fat
	259			891		*Sample size*

Appendix B   Unweighted base numbers

Table B1

Unweighted base numbers: dietary interview and seven-day dietary record by sex of respondent

Numbers

	Dietary interview	Seven-day weighed intake dietary record
Age		
Men aged (years):		
19–24	86	61
25–34	219	160
35–49	394	303
50–64	309	242
All men	1008	766
Women aged (years):		
19–24	109	78
25–34	277	211
35–49	487	379
50–64	370	290
All women	1243	958
Region		
Men		
Scotland	80	53
Northern	267	195
Central, South West and Wales	337	274
London and the South East	324	244
Women		
Scotland	111	70
Northern	341	256
Central, South West and Wales	436	350
London and the South East	355	282
Household receipt of benefits*		
Men		
Receiving benefits	145	106
Not receiving benefits	863	660
Women		
Receiving benefits	283	199
Not receiving benefits	960	759
All	2251	1724

Note: * Receipt of benefits was asked of the respondent about themselves, their partner or anyone else in the household. Benefits asked about were Working Families Tax Credit, Income Support and (Income-related) Job Seeker's Allowance.

Appendix C   Glossary of abbreviations, terms and survey definitions

Benefits (receiving)	Receipt of Working Families Tax Credit by the respondent or anyone in their household at the time of the interview, or receipt of Income Support, or (Income-related) Job Seeker's Allowance by the respondent or anyone in their household in the 14 days prior to the date of interview.
COMA	The Committee on Medical Aspects of Food and Nutrition Policy.
CAPI	Computer-assisted personal interviewing.
CASI	Computer-assisted self-interviewing. The respondent is given the opportunity to enter their responses directly on to a laptop computer. This technique is used to collect data of a sensitive or personal nature, for example, contraception.
Cum %	Cumulative percentage (of a distribution).
Deft	Design factor; *see* Notes to Tables and Appendix A.
DH	The Department of Health.
Diary sample	Respondents for whom a seven-day dietary record was obtained.
Doubly labelled water (DLW)	A method for assessing total energy expenditure, used to validate dietary assessment methods by comparison with estimated energy intake. The respondent drinks a measured dose of water labelled with the stable isotopes $^2H_2$ and ^{18}O and collects urine samples over the next 10 to 15 days. Energy expenditure is calculated from the excretion rates of the isotopes.
dna	Does not apply.
DRV	Dietary Reference Value. The term used to cover LRNI, EAR, RNI and safe intake. (*See* Department of Health. Report on Health and Social Subjects: 41. *Dietary Reference Values for Food Energy and Nutrients for the United Kingdom*. HMSO (London, 1991).)
EAR	The Estimated Average Requirement of a group of people for energy or protein or a vitamin or mineral. About half will usually need more than the EAR, and half less.
Economic activity status	Whether at the time of the interview the respondent was economically active, that is working or actively seeking work, or economically inactive, those neither working nor unemployed

	as defined by the International Labour Organisation (ILO) definition. Economically inactive includes full-time students, the retired, individuals who are looking after the home or family and those permanently unable to work due to ill health or disability.
Extrinsic sugars	Any sugar which is not contained within the cell walls of a food. Examples are sugars in honey, table sugar and lactose in milk and milk products.
GHS	The General Household Survey: a continuous, multi-purpose household survey, carried out by the Social Survey Division of ONS on behalf of a number of government departments.
HNR	Medical Research Council Human Nutrition Research, Cambridge.
Household	The standard definition used in most surveys carried out by the Social Survey Division, ONS, and comparable with the 1991 Census definition of a household was used in this survey. A household is defined as a single person or group of people who have the accommodation as their only or main residence and who either share one main meal a day or share the living accommodation. *See* McCrossan E. *A Handbook for interviewers.* HMSO (London, 1991).
HRP	Household Reference Person. This is the member of the household in whose name the accommodation is owned or rented, or is otherwise responsible for the accommodation. In households with a *sole* householder, that person is the household reference person; in households with *joint* householders, the person with the *highest income* is taken as the household reference person – if both householders have exactly the same income, the *older* is taken as the household reference person. This differs from Head of Household in that female householders with the highest income are now taken as the HRP and, in the case of joint householders, income then age (rather than sex then age) is used to define the HRP.
Intrinsic sugars	Any sugar which is contained within the cell wall of a food.
LRNI	The Lower Reference Nutrient Intake for a vitamin or mineral. An amount of nutrient that is enough for only the few people in the group who have low needs.
MAFF	The Ministry of Agriculture, Fisheries and Food.
Mean	The average value.
Median	*see* Percentiles.

MRC	The Medical Research Council.
na	Not available, not applicable.
NDNS	The National Diet and Nutrition Survey.
NFS	National Food Survey.
NMES	*See* Non-milk extrinsic sugars.
No.	Number (of cases).
Non-milk extrinsic sugars	Extrinsic sugars, except lactose in milk and milk products. Non-milk extrinsic sugars are considered to be a major contributor to the development of dental caries.
NSP	Non-starch polysaccharides. A precisely measurable component of food. A measure of 'dietary fibre'.
ONS	Office for National Statistics.
PAF	Postcode Address File: the sampling frame for the survey.
Percentiles	The percentiles of a distribution divide it into equal parts. The median of a distribution divides it into two equal parts, such that half the cases in the distribution fall (or have a value) above the median, and the other half fall (or have a value) below the median.
PSU	Primary Sampling Unit: for this survey, postcode sectors.
PUFA	Polyunsaturated fatty acid.
Region	Based on the 'Standard regions' and grouped as follows:

Scotland

Northern
North
Yorkshire and Humberside
North West

Central, South West and Wales
East Midlands
West Midlands
East Anglia
South West
Wales

London and the South East
London
South East

	The regions of England are as constituted after local government reorganisation on 1 April 1974. The regions as defined in terms of counties are listed in Chapter 2 of the Technical report online at http://www.food.gov.uk/science.
Responding sample	Respondents who completed the dietary interview and may/may not have co-operated with other components of the survey.
RNI	The Reference Nutrient Intake for protein or a vitamin or a mineral. An amount of the nutrient that is enough, or more than enough, for about 97% of the people in a group. If average intake of a group is at the RNI, then the risk of deficiency in the group is small.
sd/Std Dev	Standard deviation. An index of variability that is calculated as the square root of the variance and is expressed in the same units used to calculate the *mean* (*see* mean).
Se	Standard error. An indication of the reliability of an estimate of a population parameter, which is calculated by dividing the standard deviation of the estimate by the square root of the sample size (*see also* sd/Std Dev).
SSD	The Social Survey Division of the Office for National Statistics.
Wave; Fieldwork wave	The three-month period in which fieldwork was carried out.

Wave 1: July to September 2000
Wave 2: October to December 2000
Wave 3: January to March 2001
Wave 4: April to June 2001

WHO	World Health Organization.

Appendix D   List of tables

4:   Alcohol intake

Tables

6:   Comparison with other surveys

Tables

Appendix A: Sampling errors and statistical methods

Tables

Appendix B: Unweighted base numbers

Tables

Printed in the United Kingdom by The Stationery Office Limited
ID 142518 05/03 856845 19585